Intermediate

Quick Work

A short course in Business English

Vicki Hollett

OXFORD

1 EXCHANGING INFORMATION page 4

SECTION	INPUT TEXT	LANGUAGE WORK	TASK
Getting acquainted	Listening • business introductions	Present tenses simple/continuous/ perfect	Setting course objectives
Describing culture	Reading • corporate culture in Toyota, 3M, and FedEx	Collocations with *make* and *do*	Describing a corporate culture
Questioning costs	Listening • an interview with a manager at Hamer guitars	Checking understanding Countable and uncountable nouns	Questioning and justifying the costs of a project
Presentation skills	Listening • extracts from a presentation on Dana	Public speaking techniques Structuring talks	Delivering a short, instructive talk
Handling questions	Listening • questions about a delay in a schedule	Restating and rephrasing questions *raise* and *rise*	Handling questions from an audience on a work problem
Making a presentation	Reading • presentation messages	Revision *say* and *tell*	Making a business presentation

2 SHARING IDEAS page 16

SECTION	INPUT TEXT	LANGUAGE WORK	TASK
Generating ideas	Listening • brainstorming names for a product	Strong and weak suggestion forms Prepositions and gerunds	Brainstorming marketing ideas
Great inventions	Reading • mankind's top ten inventions	Active and passive voices	Describing an innovation in the workplace and its benefits
Evaluating ideas	Listening • an employee stock options proposal	Explaining consequences 1st vs. 2nd conditional Phrases for discussions	Evaluating new business ideas
Managing discussions	Listening • chairing a meeting	Multiword verbs	Chairing a business discussion
Holding a meeting	Reading • an article on hotel theft	Revision	Holding a meeting to solve a theft problem

3 TACKLING PROBLEMS page 24

SECTION	INPUT TEXT	LANGUAGE WORK	TASK
Reporting problems	Listening • a call reporting a packaging problem	Present perfect *should have done* Promising action	Reporting a computer access problem
Finding solutions	Reading • lessons learnt while making a movie	Past tenses simple/continuous/ perfect	Exchanging experiences of problem solving
Staffing problems	Reading • company perks	Modal verbs expressing obligation and possibility	Developing solutions to a staff turnover problem
Changing plans	Reading and listening • making and changing arrangements	Making appointments Requests, offers, and invitations Telephone expressions	Making and rearranging appointments

SECTION	INPUT TEXT	LANGUAGE WORK	TASK
Complaints	Listening • a complaint about a car rental bill	Indirect questions	Making and dealing with a complaint
Going places	Reading • a board game	Revision	Dealing with unexpected travel problems

4 PLANNING AHEAD   page 36

Presenting plans	Listening • presenting plans for a wind farm	Expressions for talking about the future	Formulating and presenting plans for reducing energy consumption
Predictions	Reading • predictions about the future of PCs	Modal verbs and expressions of possibility and probability	Gambling on the success of business ventures
Strategy	Reading • two case studies about disruptive technologies	Adjectives connotations, compounds, and antonyms	Conducting a SWOT analysis and planning a strategy
Back-up plans	Listening • changes to a website development budget	*if, when, unless, in case, until* verb – noun collocations	Preparing and explaining back-up plans
New ventures	Reading • an interview with a successful web entrepreneur	Revision	Planning and presenting a new business venture

5 RESOLVING CONFLICT   page 46

Dropping hints	Listening • negotiating the schedule for a company visit	Direct and indirect language British and American English	Negotiating a schedule for a visit
Career dilemmas	Listening and reading • career dilemmas	2nd vs. 3rd conditional 'Problem' vocabulary	Considering alternative career options
Negotiating	Listening • negotiating a distribution deal	Verbs followed by gerunds and infinitives Negotiating phrases	Negotiating agreements and solutions to business problems
Going global	Reading • a power plant's management style	Adjectives ending in *-ed* and *-ing*	Resolving conflict in an international meeting
Working across cultures	Reading • a cross-cultural questionnaire	Revision	Negotiating an agreement at a global standardization meeting

INFORMATION FILES   page 56   **LANGUAGE NOTES**   page 69

TAPESCRIPT   page 63   **GLOSSARY**   page 75

Exchanging information

CODMAN SQUARE

JUL - - 2005

In this unit you are going to study ways of asking for and presenting information. You will:

get acquainted with new business contacts

describe the culture of a business organization

question and justify costs

give a short informative talk

handle questions from an audience

deliver an effective presentation

▶ GETTING ACQUAINTED

1 Introduce yourself to some other students. Briefly tell them about yourself, your company, and your job.

2 What's the main focus of your job? Which of these things does it involve and how? What else does it involve?

planning	administration	projects	money
people	problem solving	research	

3 ⌐1.1⌐ Listen to two people being introduced and getting acquainted. What's the main focus of their jobs?

4 Compare these sentences. What tenses are they? Why did the speakers use these tenses?

a I've been working there for a couple of years now.
b We're working on the design and ordering process.
c I work with our consultants.

Which tense do we use:

1 to talk about regular and habitual activities?
2 to talk about temporary activities that are in progress now?
3 to talk about actions that began in the past and are still continuing now?

(✱) See pages 69–70 in the language notes.

5 Put the verbs in brackets in the correct tense to complete this passage.

It gives me great pleasure to introduce Ulla Eckhart. Ulla [1].............. (come) from Stockholm and she [2].............. (work) with our environmental task force since 1998. She [3].............. (currently run) a project to prevent further deforestation in Indonesia, so she [4].............. (spend) a lot of her time in planes at the moment, travelling back and forth. Although she's very busy, Ulla always [5].............. (find) time to get involved at a local level. For the last two months she [6].............. (teach) classes in Sumatra on how to build, operate, and maintain solar-powered ovens.

6 Practise making some introductions.

a Introduce two people who haven't met before.

c Introduce yourself to a visitor you're meeting at the airport.

b Introduce a speaker at a conference. Tell the audience who the speaker is and what they will be talking about.

d Introduce yourself to someone at a trade fair booth. Tell them what company you're with and why you are at the trade fair.

Task

1 Ask a partner some questions. Find out:

a how long they've been learning English
b why they're taking this course
c who they communicate with in English
d what they find most difficult about learning English.

2 What do you both need to do in English at work? Do you need to:

– attend or make presentations? (What about?)
– take part in meetings? (What about?)
– make telephone calls? (What about?)
– make plans and arrange schedules? (For what?)
– negotiate solutions to problems? (What sort of problems?)
– something else? (What?)

3 What are your priorities for this course? Decide on three key things you need to learn, then tell the class.

▶ DESCRIBING CULTURE

1 What's the company you work for like? Which of these words could you use to describe it? What other adjectives could you use?

efficient	publicly-traded	state-owned	parent
old-fashioned	multinational	medium-sized	expanding
unprofitable	well-run	dynamic	

2 What's your company culture like? Which of these qualities does your company value most highly?

– Honesty and integrity
– Teamwork and collaboration
– Hard work and commitment
– Customer service
– Action and results
– Creativity and innovation
– Something else? What?

3 Read about the three multinational companies below. What do you think their corporate cultures will value and why?

4 Read the texts about the same three companies opposite and answer these questions.

a Which company is each text about?
b What's 3M's policy towards mistakes? What's their goal regarding new products?
c What's FedEx's mission? What reward programme do they have and why?
d What is *kaizen*? What reductions has Toyota achieved?

5 Does the organization you work for do anything similar to these companies? Do you think it should? Why/Why not?

to **facilitate** to make something possible or easier
ingenious cleverly thought out or made

to **pursue** to work further on something

3M
Post-it® Notes are just one of the millions of products developed by this global manufacturer, where scientists spend 15% of their time pursuing their own ideas and researching things that interest them.

FedEx
Serving 210 countries with 650 aircraft, the world's largest express transportation company performs magic every day, moving 3.2 million packages that move the world's economy.

Toyota
The creator of the *kanban*, the ingenious materials control system that facilitates just-in-time production, this car manufacturer has led the world in production efficiency.

① **We're committed to** continuous improvement, or *kaizen*, as we call it in Japanese. This means **we're constantly looking for** ways to be more productive, more efficient, and safer. No improvement is too small for us to make and the process never stops. Sales and Manufacturing work together to do things faster too, so customers can take delivery of their new cars sooner. Following *kaizen* principles, we've achieved huge reductions in both costs and lead times.

② **It's our mission to** have a completely satisfied customer at the end of every transaction. That's not easy to do when we're shipping millions of packages around the world every day. **We have a programme that** allows managers to make extra payments to our employees on the spot. If they see someone doing something extra to take care of a customer, they can give them $100 in movie tickets or meals. In a service company you're only as good as the people performing the service.

③ **We believe** it's better to let people make mistakes than to tell them how to do their jobs and **we're well known for** encouraging our employees to take initiative. The thing is, you have to take risks if you're going to be innovative and creative. We have a goal that we have to make 30% of our revenues from products that were new in the past four years. So almost 1/3 of our income comes from products that didn't exist four years ago.

initiative action taken in order to solve a problem or make improvements
lead time the time between placing an order and receiving a product

on the spot at the same time and place as something else that's just happened
revenues total income from sales; turnover
a **transaction** a piece of business

6 Look at the expressions in blue type. Use them to make sentences about your company.

7 Look at the texts again and find some common expressions with the verbs *make* and *do*, e.g. *to make improvements, to do things faster*. Can you think of more common expressions with these verbs?

8 We use the verbs *make* and *do* in many different expressions. Here are some important meanings. Match the verbs in *italics* in the sentences below to a meaning in the diagram.

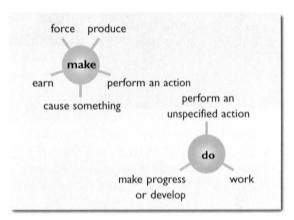

e.g. *Flying **makes** me nervous.* ..*cause something*..

a   He *makes* $200,000 a year. ....
b   It was *made* in Japan. ....
c   The police *made* me stop the car. ....
d   Can I *make* a suggestion? ....
e   What do you *do* for a living? ....
f   How are you *doing* with that report? ....
g   *Do* something! ....

Task

1 Prepare to describe the values of your company, department, or team. Make brief notes on the things that make you special.

2 Work in small groups. Take it in turns to describe your organization's values and give examples of how they operate in practice.

▶ QUESTIONING COSTS

1 Do you play the guitar? Some of the best electric guitars in the world are produced by a company called Hamer. What do you think the major costs are in making guitars like these?

2 ⟨1.2⟩ Listen to an interview with a manager from Hamer and find out:

a how many guitars the company makes a day
b how many employees it has
c how much a standard guitar costs
d why the wood is a major cost.

to **bear costs** to accept responsibility for payment
to **concentrate on** to focus your attention on something
a **craftsperson** a person who makes things skilfully, especially with their hands
a **mill** a building containing machinery to process products like wood, paper, or steel
to **pick and choose** to select very carefully, rejecting a lot
production-made made by following a process

to **represent** to be equal to
skilled having the ability and knowledge to do something well
a **surcharge** an extra amount of money that you have to pay for something
to **take pride in** something to feel pleased and proud because you do something well
to be **worth it** sensible and justified, even if it means extra expense or cost

QUICK CHECK

Talking about quantities

1 Which of these nouns are countable (C), uncountable (U), or both (U/C)?

equipment	pollution .....
information	time .....
data	space .....
fact	job .....
news	work .....
research	employee .....
person	advice .....
car	help .....
traffic	suggestion .....

2 Which of these words and phrases do we use with uncountable nouns (U), which do we use with countable nouns (C), and which can be used with both (U/C)?

a	how much	g	not much .....
b	how many	h	a .....
c	a lot of	i	a couple of .....
d	plenty of	j	a little .....
e	lots of	k	a few .....
f	not many	l	some .....

(✱) See page 73 in the language notes.

3 Underline the correct alternative in *italics* in these notes about a visit to the Hamer factory.

The manager gave me some ¹*advice/advices* about how to choose the best guitar. He also gave me lots of ²*informations/information* about Hamer's factory and the ³*equipment/equipments* they use. Everything's carved by hand, so there ⁴*wasn't/weren't* ⁵*many/much* machinery. There ⁶*was/were* very ⁷*little/few* employees too – just ten. We spent lots of ⁸*time/times* talking about the ⁹*wood/woods*, which is a major cost for Hamer. $2,000 may sound like a ¹⁰*lot/lots* to pay for a guitar, but when you consider how ¹¹*many/much* ¹²*work/works* ¹³*go/goes* into making one, it's worth it.

4 [1.2] Listen to the conversation again and notice the questions the woman asks. For each one, say whether she was asking for information or checking she understood.

5 Work with a partner. Rephrase these statements to check you've understood. Begin each time with: *So, do you mean …?* and use the words in brackets.

e.g.
A *We've concentrated on getting smaller.*
 (*wanted to?*)
B *So, do you mean you wanted to get smaller?*
A *That's right.*

a All the carving's done by hand.
 (not use any machines?)

b We only keep a third of the wood we receive.
 (reject two thirds?)

c We select the better looking, lighter weight wood.
 (interested in the appearance and the weight?)

d We have to bear the costs of shipping the wood to our factory, and then the costs of shipping it back.
 (both ways?)

e And then there's the time it takes.
 (a long time?)

f The wood selection has to be done by highly trained people
 (requires experience?)

g Selecting the right wood's very important, so we have to do it.
 (no alternative?)

6 Wood is a major cost for Hamer, but what about your company? Work in small groups. Take it in turns to interview one another about the major costs in your industries. Find out whether other students have high costs for:

a labour
b materials
c training
d R&D
e transportation
f something else. (What?)

Try to rephrase other students' answers to check you've understood.

Task

Work with a partner. The costs for your company's spring sale brochure are much higher than the original budget. You are going to discuss why. One person should look at File 3 on page 57 and the other should look at File 9 on page 59.

▶ PRESENTATION SKILLS

1 Think of the best presentation you have ever seen. What made it so good?

2 ⟦1.3⟧ Listen to three extracts from a presentation about the Dana Corporation. Do you think the presenter is doing a good job? Why/Why not?

an **asset** a useful or valuable thing that a company has or owns	to **get going** to begin
	to **implement** to start using an idea, a system, etc.
automotive connected with cars, trucks, etc.	an **overview** a short general description without much detail
brief short	
a **component** one of several parts which together make the whole of something	a **scheme** a system for organizing or doing something
to **encourage** to give hope, support, or confidence to somebody	to **submit** to propose something so it can be discussed

3 ⟦1.3⟧ Listen again and answer these questions.

Extract 1
a   What city is she in?
b   What's the subject of the talk?
c   What does the Dana Corporation do?

Extract 2
d   What's Dana's philosophy and do you agree with it?
e   How much education does Dana try to provide and do you think it's a lot?
f   What do people say about statistics and why is it funny?

Extract 3
g   How does Dana's ideas programme work?
h   How many suggestions are implemented?
i   Does your organization do anything like this and do you think it should?

4 Match the phrases in a–f from the presentation to a similar expression in 1–6 below.

a   I'd like to begin with …
b   As you can see from this table …
c   Let's turn to …
d   That brings me to my next point.
e   As I was just saying …
f   I've been asked to share some ideas on …

1   I'd like to move on to …
2   That raises the issue of …
3   Let's start with …
4   This chart shows …
5   I'm going to be talking about …
6   Going back to what I said about …

5 Which phrases in 4 are used to:
a   announce the topic of the talk?
b   start the talk?
c   refer to visuals?
d   refer back to a previous point?
e   go on to another topic?
f   link similar points?

6 [1.3] The presenter employed several public speaking techniques. Listen again and say when she does these things:

a   stresses or repeats key words and phrases
b   interacts with the audience
c   lists points in threes
d   pauses for effect
e   asks a rhetorical question (she doesn't expect an answer)
f   uses a quotation or joke.

7 The presenter said:

a   *Good morning everyone. It's great to be in Boston today. Thank you for inviting me.*

What other things can you say at the start of a presentation? And what can you say at the end?

b   *I'll be happy to take questions at the end.*

Think of another way to say this. What can you say if you want the audience to interrupt with questions?

8 Not all presentations are successful. What mistakes do speakers often make?

Task

Prepare to give a short talk to some colleagues on just one of the topics below. You can make brief notes if you wish, but don't write sentences. Just note down key words. When you're ready, take it in turns to give your talks.

–   The key ingredients of a good presentation.
–   The best presentation I ever saw.
–   Why making good presentations is important in my business.
–   Technology and visual aids – what do presenters need?
–   How to prevent nervousness before you speak in public.
–   Common mistakes presenters make.
–   Using jokes and humour in presentations.

▶ HANDLING QUESTIONS

1 What deadlines are important in your work? What happens if you don't meet them?

2 🔲1.4 Listen to a manager dealing with questions from a sales team at a software company and answer these questions.

a   What deadline was missed?

b   What was the original ship date and what is the new one?

c   What caused the delay?

d   Have any other releases been delayed?

e   Why are development schedules getting longer?

f   What are they doing about this problem?

Do you think he handles the questions well? Why/Why not?

a **deadline** a time or date before which something must be done	a **short cut** a quicker, easier, or more direct way to do something
a **release** something made available to the public, e.g. *press release, software release*	**simultaneously** at the same time
a **ship date** the date on which a product is shipped	a **step** one action in a series of actions

3 🔲1.4 Listen again and identify questions with a similar meaning to the following.

a   When will it be shipped?

b   Could you say that again?

c   Why is this problem arising?

d   Do you mean in this particular case, or in general?

e   Is the situation deteriorating?

f   Whose fault is it?

g   How are you tackling this problem?

4 Sometimes the questions people ask aren't very clear. Which of these phrases indicate you didn't hear a question and which indicate you didn't understand what the questioner meant?

a   Sorry, what was that?

b   I'm afraid I'm not following you.

c   Could you be a little more specific?

d   I didn't catch that.

e   One more time, please.

f   Can you give me an example?

g   I'm not quite sure what you're getting at.

5 Sometimes we might want to ignore a question and ask one we'd prefer to answer. Change these questions. Start with: *I think the important question is …* and use the words in brackets.

e.g.

A   *Who's responsible for this problem? (what/do about it?)*

B   *I think the important question is what are we doing about it.*

a   Whose fault is it?
    (how/solve the problem)

b   Why haven't you done anything about it?
    (what/going to do about it)

c   How much damage has been done?
    (how/avoid long term damage)

d   What caused this problem?
    (what/do to stop it happening again)

e   Who made this mistake?
    (what/learn from this mistake)

QUICK CHECK

raise and *rise*

1   Are *raise* and *rise* regular or irregular verbs?

2   Complete these sentences with the correct form of *raise* or *rise*.

   a   I'd like to .... a point here.

   b   Do you think these costs will continue to ....?

   c   We need to .... our standards.

   d   There's no need to .... your voice.

3   Which explanation is *raise* and which is *rise*?

   a   to move upward, to become higher, or to increase

   b   to lift something, to increase something, or make something stronger

6 Here are some phrases you can use to give
yourself more time to think when you're
replying to questions. Match each phrase to the
most appropriate thought.

a That's tough to answer
in a few words.

b I couldn't have explained
that properly.

c I'm afraid I don't know
the answer to that.

d Perhaps Mrs Murphy
could answer that.

e Let me repeat what I said
about that earlier.

f I'm very glad you raised
that point.

g That's a very good
question.

1 Oh, why did you have to
ask me that?

2 You seem to be important
and I'd like you on my side.

3 We'll run out of time if I
answer that now.

4 It's not my field so I'll
pass the buck.

5 Oh good! There's something
else I want to say about this.

6 Or perhaps you didn't
listen?

7 And pay attention this
time!

Task

1 Think of a problem you face in your
workplace. You can choose one from this list or
think of another.

– tighter and tighter deadlines
– falling demand
– heavy competition
– corruption
– poor training
– unreliable suppliers
– security
– labour shortages
– rising costs
– government legislation

2 Take it in turns to stand up and take
questions from the class about your problem.
You can announce what the problem is, for
example, *falling demand*. After that, you should
only answer questions. The class should ask as
many questions as they can to find out:

– exactly what the problem is
– what causes it
– what effects it has
– whether it's getting better or worse
– what alternative solutions there are
– what (if anything) is being done about it.

▶ MAKING A PRESENTATION

1 Look at these tips for presenters. Which ones do you think are most useful? Can you think of any more to add?

> – Practise, practise, practise.
> – Check all the equipment is working before you start.
> – Don't read your speech off a page. Use brief notes.
> – Say what you're going to say, say it, and then say what you've said.
> – Maintain eye contact with your audience.
> – Be enthusiastic.
> – KISS – keep it short and simple.
> – Don't rush it. Speak slowly and clearly.

2 What kinds of talks or presentations do you make in your job? Who are the audiences and what are the talks about? What messages do you need to convey?

3 Match these different messages to the most probable audience.

Audience	Message
a shareholders	1 'We'll do whatever it takes to make you happy.'
b suppliers	
c potential customers	2 'Trust us. We can make your money grow.'
d potential recruits	3 'Believe in the product and you'll close the deals.'
e a sales team	
	4 'We provide an excellent environment for career development.'
	5 'If you meet our needs, you'll earn our loyalty.'

4 In what ways might you change your presentation style for different audiences? Imagine you had to give a technical presentation on a new product. Which of these things might you include for an audience of engineers, which might you include for an audience of senior managers, and which might you include for both?

a a broad overview and summaries
b a detailed examination and analysis of data
c theory
d jargon and technical terms
e a focus on costs, benefits, and future business potential
f statistics, mathematical equations, charts and diagrams with lots of data
g graphs showing general trends and attractive PowerPoint® slides

QUICK CHECK

say and *tell*

Do we *say* or *tell*:

a   someone something?
b   something?
c   what happened?
d   everyone what happened?
e   we're sorry to someone?
f   'hello'?
g   someone what to do?
h   someone our phone number?
i   our phone number loudly and clearly?
j   the truth?
k   someone a secret?

(✳)   See page 74 in the language notes.

5   Prepare to give a short talk to an audience. First, decide on the audience you will address. Choose one of these groups or invent your own. *Don't* tell anyone what audience you've chosen – keep it secret.

–   senior management
–   a team of your colleagues
–   potential customers
–   potential suppliers
–   new recruits
–   school children who are visiting your company
–   someone else (who?)

6   Think about the content of your talk. What is your message? What does your audience want or need to know? Write down the key point you want to get across using a maximum of ten words.

7   Now prepare what you're going to say. Make brief notes, if you like, but don't write the whole talk. Just write key words to remind yourself of what you wanted to say. (The KISS principle usually works best.)

8   Work in small groups. Take it in turns to give your presentations and deal with questions from the audience. While each person is speaking, the other students should think about:

–   who the audience could be
–   what the message is
–   good questions to ask.

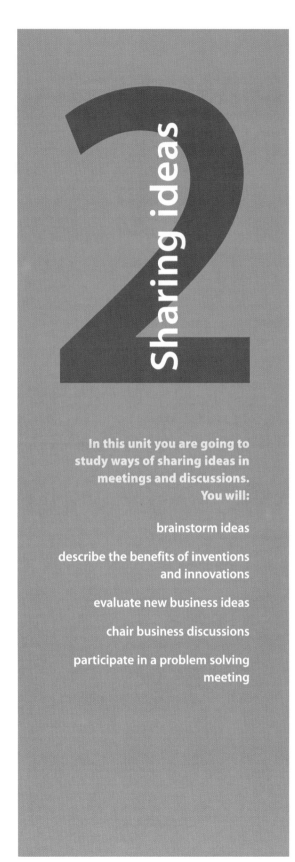

2

Sharing ideas

In this unit you are going to study ways of sharing ideas in meetings and discussions. You will:

brainstorm ideas

describe the benefits of inventions and innovations

evaluate new business ideas

chair business discussions

participate in a problem solving meeting

▶ GENERATING IDEAS

1 In what ways do you have to be creative in your job? Do you ever hold brainstorming meetings to come up with ideas? How are they different to normal meetings? Which of these things would you *not* do in a brainstorming meeting?

a Take notes.
b Judge ideas one by one, as people think of them.
c Encourage wild ideas.
d Follow an agenda.
e Ask the chair for permission to speak.
f Build on the ideas of others.

2 2.1 Listen to a meeting where people are brainstorming ideas for the name of a new product. Find out what kind of product it is.

to **appoint** someone to choose somebody for a job **baldness** having little or no hair on the head to **convey** to communicate something; to make ideas, thoughts, or feelings known	to **inspire** to give somebody a feeling of being able to do something good a **remedy** something that solves a problem to **restore** to put something back into it's original condition

3 2.1 Listen again and answer these questions.

a What does Yumi offer to do at the beginning?
b What different messages do they want the name to convey?
c Why does the woman want to hear Roberto's ideas?
d What executive, medical, and masculine names do they think of?
e What name does Peter suggest?

4 2.1 They use a lot of different phrases and expressions to make suggestions. Listen again and identify as many as you can.

5 Study these common phrases for making suggestions.

I think we should ...   *Is it a good idea ...?*
We could ...   *How about ...?*
We'd better ...

a Which are more forceful?
b Which phrase is followed by a gerund (an *-ing* form)?
c Which phrase is followed by a full infinitive form (*to do*)?
d What's the negative form of *We'd better ...*? What word is shortened to *'d*?
e What's the negative form of *I think we should ...*? What's the question form?

6 Look at these different ways of reacting to ideas. Which are positive, which are negative, and which could be either, depending on how they are said?

a What a great idea!
b It won't work.
c It might work.
d It's worth a try.
e Good thinking!
f It's an interesting idea.

7 Work in small groups. You are all colleagues. Brainstorm different solutions to these problems.

a You want to learn English more quickly. What different things can you do together?
b The instruction manual for your new robot is written in a language you don't know.
c Some valuable documents have to be delivered to a client's office in New York by tomorrow evening. How can you get them there?
d A hacker is threatening to bring down your computer system if you don't pay them $1 million by six o' clock this evening.
e You want to increase your income. How can you do it?

Task

Work in small groups. You work for a company that produces vitamins and other dietary supplements, which you sell by mail order. You have developed a pill that improves people's memories. Hold a meeting to generate some marketing ideas. Discuss these questions.

a What sort of people will want to buy this product and why?
b What are the best marketing and advertising media to use?
c What image do you want the product to have?
d What name should it have?
e What sales slogan could you use?
f What packaging could it have?

▶ GREAT INVENTIONS

1 The telephone, the electric light bulb, planes, the zip fastener – all these inventions have benefited people's lives. Brainstorm as many of mankind's greatest inventions as you can.

2 The names of inventions are missing in the article on the opposite page. Read it and work out what they are. Check your answers in File 2 on page 56.

an **alloy** a metal formed from a mixture of metals or of metals and other substances	**miniaturization** the act of making things on a much smaller scale
to **amplify** to make louder	to **minimize** to make something as small as possible
an **epidemic** the rapid spread of a disease or illness in an area	
an **impact** an effect	to **transform** to change something
to **mass produce** produce in large quantities	**vital** very important or necessary

3 Look at the sentences and phrases that are in *italics* in the text. Which ones are active and which are passive? Underline the passives. Now compare the active and passive sentences. Which ones describe:

a   what the inventions have done?
b   what has happened to the inventions?

When do we use passives in English?

(✱)   See page 73 in the language notes.

4 What's the best way of continuing after the sentences below? Choose the best alternative (1 or 2). Think about whether you're saying what things do or what has happened to them.

a   Have you seen our new robot?
  1   People in Taiwan made it.
  2   It was made in Taiwan.
b   I have a new pager.
  1   It can receive e-mail messages.
  2   E-mail messages can be received.
c   This ceiling fan is top of the range.
  1   It's operated by remote control.
  2   Remote controls operate it.

d   The new model isn't ready for release.
  1   Scientists are still testing it.
  2   It's still being tested.
e   We're using a telephone call routing system.
  1   The cheapest carrier is located by it.
  2   It locates the cheapest carrier.
f   The new inventory management system is excellent.
  1   It's enabled us to cut costs.
  2   We've been enabled to cut costs.

5 Work with a partner. You're going to describe the benefits of some more inventions. One person should look at File 4 on page 57 and the other should look at File 6 on page 58.

Task

1 Think of an invention or innovation that has changed the way you work or do business. It might be new software, new equipment, or a new work system. Prepare to tell some other students about it. Make notes in the chart below.

	Example	Your innovation
What it is	A web-based purchasing system.	
How it works	Distributes requests for price quotations, locates all the suppliers qualified to manufacture a particular product or part, collects bids.	
Other things you know about it	Developed in Germany. Installed on our computer system last year.	
The benefits it's brought	Allows us to buy materials at the lowest price – enables faster communications.	

2 When you're ready, work in small groups. Tell one another about your innovations and answer questions.

Focus Magazine's top ten inventions

a ....

Of course this has existed since the earliest of times, but humans had no way of creating it themselves until just 9,000 years ago. Its impact on human development is incalculable. *It kept early humans warm* and enabled them to cook and make new materials – such as alloys from metal.

b ....

Invented at Bell laboratories in the US, this device is basically just a tiny sandwich of special metals. But it can amplify the very weakest of signals and *it made miniaturization possible.* It plays a vital role in today's electronics and computer industries.

c ....

Nobody knows when this was invented, though Sumerians had them 5,500 years ago. They are the perfect shape for minimizing contact with other surfaces and *they are used everywhere* – from inside computers to roller skates.

d ....

It began in 1969 with some scientists in the US military linking together a few computers on different sites. And *now it* combines more than 10 million host computers and enables astonishing numbers of people all over the world to link up and communicate with one another.

e ....

This was invented in Germany by Johannes Gutenburg around 1450, and it enabled people to mass produce books for the first time. At last the world had a way of taking knowledge out of the control of a few and putting it into the hands of many.

f ....

When it was first invented by Theodore Maiman in 1960, most people had no idea how useful this invention would be. *It was even described as 'a solution looking for a problem'.* But they are now employed in all sorts of applications, ranging from metal cutters to CD players (where the beam of light reads the information off the disc).

g ....

No one person can claim all the credit for this invention. Mathematicians such as Charles Babbage, Alan Turing, and Johnny Von Neumann laid the foundations, but we have to thank other people such as Bill Gates too. *It allows humans to do superhuman things.*

h ....

Not cleaning his laboratory led Alexander Fleming to discover the first of these valuable bacteria. But it was the Australian and German scientists, Howard Florey and Ernst Chain who identified penicillin *and since then, new forms have been developed* that have saved millions of lives.

i ....

Before this was invented, death through cholera and other epidemics was a common danger in cities. Without clean water supplies people couldn't live and work together safely. *This invention has enabled businesses to grow,* and capitalism to transform the modern world.

j ....

Scottish physicist James Clerk Maxwell predicted it was possible in 1862, but it was the Italian inventor Marconi who turned it into a worldwide communications medium. *Without it, the more sophisticated technologies of TV, satellites, and cell phones might never have been invented.*

▶ EVALUATING IDEAS

1 [2.2] Listen to someone making a proposal. Do you think it's a good idea? Could it work in your organization?

committed giving a lot of your time and attention to something because you think it is right or important to **dilute** to make weaker	a **share** one of the equal parts into which the ownership of a company is divided **stock** shares in a company that people can buy and sell **viable** will be successful

2 [2.2] Listen to the proposal again. What common expressions does he use to talk about consequences? Complete these sentences.

a Not just the managers – .... the mail boy should get some and the tea lady should get some.
b .... our stock will be wider spread.
c .... everyone feel more committed.
d .... they'll care more and think about the value of what they're doing.
e .... we'll see huge benefits.

3 Match the first parts of these proposals to the endings 1–5. Which ones could be useful ideas in your company? Can you suggest some alternative endings?

a We should implement a dress code so ...
b People should stop sending copies of e-mails to half the company. Then ...
c I'm pleased we're all doing this time management course. It's going to make ...
d We should experiment with holding meetings standing up. That way ...
e Enclosing lottery tickets in our direct mail shots to customers is a great idea. It means ...

1 ... our mail boxes won't get filled up with messages that don't concern us.
2 ... they won't throw them away.
3 ... they won't go on for too long.
4 ... we make a better impression on our customers.
5 ... us more efficient.

4 [2.2] [2.3] Listen to the proposal again, then listen to someone responding to it. Which person do you agree with?

5 [2.3] Listen again and finish these sentences?

a *If we issued more shares, ...*
b *If people aren't working hard enough, ...*

Compare the two sentences. Which one describes something she thinks is:

1 possible?
2 possible in theory, but unlikely to happen in practice?

What tenses did she use?

(✱) **See pages 71–72 in the language notes.**

6 Here are some suggestions for improving your company's performance. Are they things that:

– your company could do? (Write: *1*)
– your company could do, but is unlikely to do? (Write: *2*)

a Invest heavily in e-commerce. ....
b Outsource more work. ....
c Increase the research budget. ....
d Cut the training budget. ....
e Demand larger discounts from suppliers. ....
f Cancel the staff Christmas party. ....
g Freeze wages and salaries. ....
h Promote you to a higher position. ....
i Make you the CEO. ....

7 Now say what will/would happen if the ideas in 6 are/were implemented. Remember to use the appropriate conditional form, depending on how certain you feel.

e.g.
If we invest heavily in e-commerce, we'll stay competitive. (I think we could invest.)
If we invested heavily in e-commerce, it'd be a waste of money, time, and effort. (I think we're unlikely to invest.)

Task

Here are some new business ideas some companies have been experimenting with. Read about them and discuss these points.

a Why have these companies done these things? What possible benefits could they have? What do you think of these ideas?

b Do you do anything similar in your organization already? Could you implement something similar? What would the results be?

an **animator** someone whose job it is to make pictures appear to move **Inc** (abbreviation) incorporated a **nap** a short sleep **preferential** giving or showing better treatment to one person or group than to others	to **price** to set the price of something to **run to** to add up to; to total a **temp** a temporary member of staff a **tent** a shelter made of cloth

Pricing

Coca-Cola has been experimenting with a smart Coke machine that would price Coke higher on a hot day and at a lower price on a cold day. Little Caesars was thinking of pricing the same pizza at $10 at noon and $8 at 3 p.m.

Voicemail and automated calls

Cablevision Systems issued a memo to its employees declaring that 'all calls must go to a human voice' and ordered a shutdown of the company's automated call answering system. The company has hired temps so that live people answer all calls.

Foreign labour

Animation Magic Inc. hired artists in Russia to work as computer animators for about $2,100 a year. Annual salaries for comparable artists in the United States would have run to $60,000–$80,000.

Naps

Taking a nap at the office is gaining acceptance in some workplaces. Gould Evans Goodman Associates, an architectural firm in Kansas City, provides tents for naps in its offices. Yarde Metals, a Connecticut-based metals distributor, also has space for about twenty-five workers to take naps in its new facility.

Job change

Two General Motors divisions, Oldsmobile and GMC truck, asked their employees to reapply for their jobs. The employees had to compete for their jobs with other outside applicants and they received no preferential treatment. GM said the jobs had changed so much, workers needed new skills to do them.

▶ MANAGING DISCUSSIONS

1 What are the ingredients for a successful meeting? How important is the chairperson? What different tasks do they need to perform?

2 ☐2.4 Listen to three extracts from a meeting. What tasks does the chairperson perform in each one? Do you think they chair the meeting well?

to **aim** to intend to achieve something	to be **overdrawn** having spent more money than you have in your bank account
to **fill** someone **in** to give someone information about something	a **quote** (abbreviation) a quotation; a price estimate
to **get through** something to complete; to finish	to **work** something **out** to find the answer to something
	wrapped up finished

3 Here are some tasks a chairperson often performs. Match each one to an appropriate expression 1–9 below.

a explains the objectives of the meeting
b sets a target time for the meeting to finish
c calls on people to speak
d collects people's opinions
e checks what people mean if it isn't clear
f stops people talking too long
g moves through the agenda
h summarizes the decisions made
i allocates tasks and sets deadlines

1 So, are you saying ...?
2 OK, so we've agreed that we'll ...
3 We need to decide what we're going to do about ...
4 OK, let's turn to item three, which is ...
5 I'm aiming to get through this by eleven thirty.
6 Could you get some quotes by next Tuesday, Martin?
7 How do you feel about this, Martin?
8 Heather, could you fill us in on ...
9 Yes thanks, Stephen. Perhaps we could come back to this later if we have time.

4 ☐2.4 Listen to the extracts again. Identify the phrases in 3 that the chairperson uses. Does she use any other useful phrases?

5 Here are some more things a chairperson might say. Look at the multiword verbs in *italics* and match each one to a meaning in this list.

handle   consider   go faster   continue   rely on
discuss   delay   cause

a We're listening. Please *go on*.
b Let's *think about* this.
c Let's not *go into* this now.
d It'll *set* us *back*.
e We need to *speed up* if we're going to finish by three.
f What's *brought* this problem *about*?
g Who's going to *deal with* this?
h Can I *count on* everyone's support?

Task

Work in small groups and hold a short meeting. Take it in turns to be the chairperson and deal with one of the items on the agenda below. As chairperson, remember to:

– explain the objective of the discussion
– collect everyone's opinions
– get agreement on what's to be done
– decide who will do it and when by.

Agenda

---

1 Providing more IT training for employees.

2 Recruiting a new security officer.

3 Laying off the company cleaners and outsourcing the work.

4 Arrangements for the employee summer party.

▶ HOLDING A MEETING

1 For many hotels, theft is a serious problem. What items do people steal from hotels? Brainstorm some ideas then read the article below and find out.

Hotel theft

Every twelve seconds, somebody steals a towel from a Holiday Inn hotel. A survey of British hotels found pictures, hair dryers, and kettles were also popular targets for theft. Over a period of four years, one hotel in Surrey, England lost 13 coffee percolators, 41 bathroom mugs, 350 knives, forks, and spoons, 10 kettles, 5 crystal chandeliers, 236 sheets, 180 pillow cases, 426 towels, 60 ashtrays, 283 toilet rolls, 1 toilet seat, and a bed. The strange thing was nobody noticed. The police only discovered the thefts when they searched the home of one of the hotel's cleaners and found all the items stored away, unused.

2 Work in small groups. You're the managers of a hotel and you have a problem with theft. You're not sure who is responsible – hotel staff or guests – but it's probably both. Brainstorm ideas for solving the problem. Think of as many ideas as you can. Don't worry if they are good or bad solutions yet, just think of ideas. Appoint someone to make notes.

3 Here are some ideas for dealing with the problem. Did you think of them?

- Search everyone before they leave the building.

- Never employ anyone with a criminal record.

- Employ more security staff.

- Install security cameras in the rooms.

- Make sure your cleaners never work alone. Put them in teams of two or three.

- When guests go out, look in their bags to see if they have stolen anything.

- Conduct regular stock checks.

- Fix ashtrays to the furniture.

- Ask guests to pay a deposit before you give them a TV or telephone.

- When guests check out, ask them to wait a few minutes while you check their rooms.

4 Prepare to hold a meeting to decide how to deal with the problem of theft in your hotel. Look through all the ideas you thought of and those in 3, and draw up an agenda. Decide who will introduce the discussion on each agenda point at the meeting.

5 Decide whether to elect a chairperson and if so who it will be.

6 Hold your meeting and draw up an action plan. Decide what to do, who will do it, and when by.

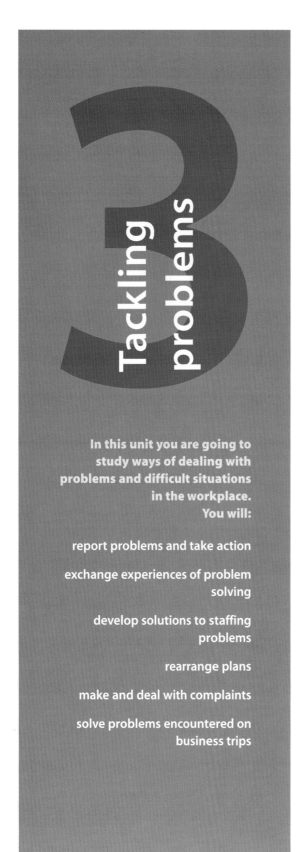

3

Tackling problems

In this unit you are going to study ways of dealing with problems and difficult situations in the workplace. You will:

report problems and take action

exchange experiences of problem solving

develop solutions to staffing problems

rearrange plans

make and deal with complaints

solve problems encountered on business trips

REPORTING PROBLEMS

1 Where do you travel on business? How do you keep in contact with your office when you're out of town?

2 3.1 Gary works for an American company that makes brake pads for cars. He's currently in Saudi Arabia, visiting customers. Listen to his phone call to a colleague back home. What problem is he reporting?

apparently according to what people say	a **pallet** a flat wooden platform for carrying goods
a **brake pad** part of a car's braking system which causes the car to slow down or stop	to be **up to** something to be doing something unknown – possibly something bad

3 Now study what he said. Can you work out what Debbie said (...) ?

Debbie? Hi, it's Gary in Jeddah. (...) Fine thanks, but we've got a problem with our brake pads. (...) I visited the plant where they're being installed today and they're complaining about them. (...) No, they work fine. It's the way they're packed. It's difficult for the guys on the line to get them off the pallets and do their job. (...) For a couple of weeks. They were all right before that apparently. Could you find out what our packaging people have been up to and let me know? (...) Good, and please get back to me as soon as you can. (...) It's eleven o'clock at night. I'm nine hours ahead of you here. (...) The Holiday Inn. The number's: 966 2 631 4000. I'm in room 664. (...) Great, thanks Debbie.

4 3.2 Now listen to the whole conversation and check your answers. What questions did Debbie ask? What did she promise to do?

7 Look at some of the things Debbie said. What tenses did she use?

*Logistics **changed** the stacking method last month.*
*They **found** a way to get more brake pads on to the pallets.*
*They**'ve agreed** to change back to the old system.*
*I**'ve set up** a meeting.*

The sentences all describe events that happened in the past so why does she use different tenses? Which tenses do we use when we're interested in:

a   what happened in the past?
b   the current results of a past action?

Now look at something Gary said:

They should've checked with the customer first.

Did Logistics check with the customer? What does he mean by *first*?

(✳)   See page 70 in the language notes.

8 Work with a partner. Update one another on your progress at work. Tell your partner:

a   some of the jobs you've done this week
b   some of the jobs you should have done, but haven't. Explain why you haven't done them.

5 Here are some things we might promise to do when people have a problem.

a   I'll find out what's going on.
b   I'll get back to you.
c   I'll let you know.
d   I'll take care of it.
e   I'll look into it and work something out.

Which one means you'll:

1   tell them something?
2   call them later with an answer?
3   investigate and find an answer?
4   organize or arrange a solution?
5   discover what's happening?

6 ⌐3.3⌐ Now listen to the call Debbie made to Gary later that night.

a   What change did Logistics make and why?
b   What should have happened?
c   What has Debbie done about it?

to **stack**   to put things neatly in a pile

Task

Call 1   You're visiting the UK on business and you've been trying to access your company's computer system via the web. You had no problems doing this yesterday, but today you are getting the message 'access denied'. Call a colleague, ask them to contact your IT department and find out what's going on.

Work with a partner and act out two telephone calls. One person should read the information here and the other should read the information in File 10 on page 60.

Call 2   Your partner calls you back. Find out what caused the problem, what's been done about it, and discuss what should have happened.

▶ FINDING SOLUTIONS

1 Read the story below about a problem a film producer had. What's the moral of the story? What can it tell us about how to solve problems?

2 Ask and answer these questions with another student.

a What different logistical problems did the film producer have with *Gorillas in the Mist*?

b Why was the studio worried?

c What was the biggest problem he faced?

d How did he solve it?

3 What do you think he learnt from the experience? Look at File 7 on page 58 to see if you are right.

an **altitude** a height above sea level
to **go over budget** to spend more money than planned or agreed
logistics the organization of supplies and services for a complex operation

a **nightmare** an unpleasant or frightening experience
on the verge of doing something very near to doing something; near the start of something
to **shelve** to decide not to continue with a plan

What if?

'Sometimes life is all about solving problems and in the movie business there seems to be one around every corner. I had a very valuable lesson in how to tackle problems once from a young female trainee. It happened while I was producing the movie *Gorillas in the Mist* and she actually saved the movie from being shelved by the studio.

The logistics of *Gorillas in the Mist* had become a nightmare. We wanted to film at a very high altitude of 11,000 feet in the middle of the jungle in Rwanda – then on the verge of a revolution – and to use more than 200 animals. The Warner Brothers Studio was financing the movie and it was worried that we would go over budget. But our biggest problem was that the story required the gorillas to do what we wrote – in other words, to "act".

We called an emergency meeting to solve these problems. In the middle of it, the young trainee asked, "What if you let the gorillas write the story?" Everyone laughed and wondered what she was doing in a meeting with experienced film-makers.

Hours later, someone casually asked her what she had meant. She said, "What if you sent a really good cinematographer into the jungle with a ton of film to shoot the gorillas? Then you could write a story around what the gorillas did on film." It was a brilliant idea. We did exactly what she suggested, and we made the movie for $20 million – half of the original budget!'

4 Underline the verbs in these sentences. What tenses are they and why did the writer use these tenses?

It happened while I was producing the movie, Gorillas in the Mist.
Hours later, someone casually asked her what she had meant.

Which tense is used:

a   to show that one event happened before another in the past?
b   to set the scene and describe the circumstances of a past event?

Find more examples of these tenses in the story.

(✳)   See page 69 in the language notes.

5   Read another film producer's story and put the verbs in brackets into the correct tense. (More than one answer may be possible.)

Task

1   Prepare to tell some other students a similar story from your experience. Think about:

a   a memorable learning experience you had and how it arose (what were the circumstances?)
b   what you did and what happened as a result
c   what you learnt from the experience.

Make brief notes if you like, but don't write sentences, just write key words.

2   When you're ready, work in pairs or small groups and take it in turns to tell your stories. What can you learn from these experiences about solving problems?

People don't like change, but change can be good for business. I first ^{1}.............. (learn) this lesson while I ^{2}.............. (make) a promotional film for the Phelps Dodge Copper Corporation. It ^{3}.............. (include) some tricky scenes at copper mines that ^{4}.............. (involve) explosive experts and technicians.

My favourite shot had an actor standing in front of a mine, wearing a hard hat. He ^{5}.............. (talk) about how we get copper out of the ground, when suddenly, there ^{6}.............. (be) a spectacular explosion behind him. The timing was perfect.

But when the Board of Directors ^{7}..............

(see) the finished film, they didn't like the actor. The Board ^{8}.............. (approve) the script before we started filming and their advertising agency ^{9}.............. (select) the actor, so it wasn't my fault. But I had to negotiate a bigger budget and shoot a lot of scenes again.

I was very upset about it until several months later when I ^{10}.............. (add up) the numbers and discovered that we ^{11}.............. (made) more profit on the re-shoots than we ^{12}.............. (made) on the original film.

Change is inevitable so it's better to accept that there will be change in any project and try to make money from it.

| **copper** a common reddish-brown metal | **inevitable** cannot be avoided or prevented from happening |

▶ STAFFING PROBLEMS

1 What's the unemployment rate in your country? Does your company have problems finding good employees? Are there any jobs that are particularly hard to fill? Does your company manage to keep its employees – is the staff turnover high or low?

2 Read about some of the perks and benefits offered by companies in America. Which perks would you like to have?

a **cubicle** a small box-like compartment that people work in
a **dress code** standards or guidelines for the clothes that people can wear
to be **entitled to** having the right to have or do something
a **futon** a Japanese mattress used as a bed
in short supply a situation where there isn't enough of something

a **nap** a short sleep
to **offend** to upset; to hurt
a **perk** a benefit
recognition appreciation and acknowledgement for an achievement or ability
a **referral** passing on a contact for someone else to deal with
reimbursement repayment of a cost

Top perks

Employees are the most important asset most companies have, which can be a problem when labour's in short supply. Good employees should receive recognition, but not everyone can be promoted and salary increases aren't always enough. So how can companies attract and keep the best employees? Here's what some of the best companies to work for in America are doing.

- Flexible working hours are popular everywhere and at the software company WRQ 95% of the staff have them. The company also has a nap room with futons and on-site massages.
- At the insurance company AFLAC employees *can* have 12 weeks off with full pay if they *need to* care for a sick husband, wife, child, or parent.
- If you get married while you're working for the credit card company MBNA, you're entitled to an extra week of vacation.
- You'*ve got to* pay a lot of money if you want to go to school in the US. But it's not so bad if you work for the US division of the Finnish company Nokia. Its tuition reimbursement can reach $5,000.
- Employees at CDW Computer Centres get free ice-cream in the summer and fruit and bagels every Tuesday and Thursday.
- Staff members *don't need to* 'perform work that offends their personal principles' at the accounting firm Plante and Moran.
- If you want to work for Microsoft, you *should* get to know someone who works there – 40% of recruits come from employee referrals.
- You *don't have to* worry about keeping up with your housework if you work for the printing company Valassis Communications. They provide employees with discounts on maid services and ready-to-heat meals.
- The CEO at Intel *has to* work in a cubicle like everybody else, and there are no reserved parking spaces.
- The dress code is casual at Sun Microsystems. As CEO Scott McNealy puts it: 'The only dress code is that you *must.*'

3 Work with a partner and answer these questions.

a Why do these companies provide such valuable perks?
b What can tired workers at WRQ do?
c What do employees have to do to qualify for an extra week of vacation at MBNA?
d Which company should you try to work for if you want to study and why?
e What must you do if you work for Sun Microsystems? What don't you have to do?
f Does your company do anything similar to the ones in the article?

4 Look at the words and expressions in *italics* in the article. Which ones do we use to talk about things that:

a people are obliged to do or ought to do?
b aren't necessary?
c are possible?

5 Which of these verbs express strong obligation? Which express weaker obligation?

have to   must   should   ought to   need to   have got to

What are the negative forms of these verbs? Which negative forms do we use to talk about things that are:

a forbidden or prohibited?
b not necessary?

(✳) See page 71 in the language notes.

6 Use the verbs in 5 above to explain your company's regulations regarding:

– hours of work, lunch and coffee breaks
– health, sickness, and maternity benefits
– vacation time
– training
– dress code.

7 Benefits cost money. What benefits do you think your company should and shouldn't offer its employees and why?

Task

You work for a large furniture retail organization and your staff turnover has risen from 16% to 26% over the last three years. It's particularly high among shop floor workers and this is a very expensive problem. The average cost of replacing a member of staff is equivalent to a whole year's salary.

1 You have conducted a study to find out why employees leave and the results are below. Take a few minutes to study the results. Why are people leaving and what can you do about this?

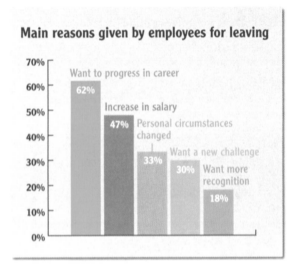

Main reasons given by employees for leaving

- Want to progress in career — 62%
- Increase in salary — 47%
- Personal circumstances changed — 33%
- Want a new challenge — 30%
- Want more recognition — 18%

2 You're going to hold a meeting to decide what to do about your staff turnover problem. Prepare some proposals to make. You might like to suggest:

– providing more opportunities for career progression (why and how?)
– increasing salaries (why and how?)
– providing more training (why and what?)
– offering more perks/benefits (why and what?)
– something else (what and why?).

3 Work in small groups and hold the meeting. Take it in turns to present your proposals and together decide what to do.

▶ CHANGING PLANS

1 Who do you talk to in English on the phone? What about?

Exchanging information on the phone

1 What different things can we say:

   a to ask a caller to wait?

   b to explain why a colleague is not available?

   c to check we're calling someone at a convenient time?

   d to indicate we want to finish a call?

   e at the end of a call?

2 Look at these notes and find an example of:

   a a capital letter   f lower case letters

   b a hyphen   g a colon

   c an underscore   h a forward slash

   d country code   i an area code

   e an 'at' symbol   j a dot

Mr Østen Åkesson from Oslo.

+47 22 43 88 15

dr_j_heggerty@hotmail.com

http://www.oup-usa.org/esl

If you needed to dictate this information over the phone, how should you say it?

2 [3.4] Listen to an answering machine message and find out how you can contact Peter Clark.

3 How can people contact you when you're not at your desk? Prepare a similar message that you could leave on your answering machine and then say it aloud or record it.

4 [3.5] Peter had a message from a potential customer. Listen and make notes about the caller, their contact details, and the message.

5 [3.6] Peter responded to the message. Here's his conversation with Carmen, but only the first and last sentences are in the correct order. Number the other boxes in the correct order and read it with a partner. Then listen and check your answers.

[1] Hello Ms Santez, this is Peter Clark of Gencia returning your call.

[ ] Could you? That would make things a lot easier for me.

[ ] Ah, thank you for getting back to me so quickly. I'm sorry about Friday.

[ ] No problem. When would be good for you?

[ ] Excellent. And would you mind coming to my hotel? I could book a meeting room.

[ ] How are you fixed for Tuesday afternoon – say two o'clock?

[ ] I'd love to but my schedule's very tight as I'm leaving New York on Wednesday. Do you mind if I don't come down to Washington?

[ ] Oh that's all right. Would you like to reschedule?

[ ] That's fine for me.

[ ] Would you like me to come up to New York instead?

[11] That's great. I'll look forward to seeing you at the Marriott at two o'clock on Tuesday then.

6 Here are some of the expressions they used to reschedule. Can you think of other ways to say these things?

a   I'm afraid I can't make our meeting on Friday.
b   When would be good for you?
c   How are you fixed for Tuesday afternoon?
d   That's fine for me.

7 Look at these phrases from the conversation.

a   Would you like to ...?
b   Do you mind if I ...?
c   Would you like me to ...?
d   Would you mind (-ing) ...?

Which one do we use to:

1   ask people to do things for us?
2   ask for permission to do things ourselves?
3   invite people to do things with us?
4   offer to do things for other people?

These phrases are all quite formal. What other phrases could you use with people you know well? How could you reply to phrases like these?

8 Practise the phrases with a partner. Follow these instructions.

Conversation 1

A   Think of somewhere to go this weekend and invite B to come with you.

B   Ask A to tell you more about it.

A   Tell B about it.

B   Ask if you can bring someone else along with you.

A   Agree and fix a time and place to meet.

Conversation 2

B   Something has come up and you can't make it. Explain the problem to A.

A   Offer to reschedule.

B   Say thank you and arrange another time.

Task

Work with a partner. One person should use the information below and the other should use the information in File 14 on page 61.

Here's your diary for next week.

Call 1 Your partner's company makes robots and you're interested in buying some. Call and arrange an appointment to find out more about their products.

Call 2 Your partner returns your call. You'd like to visit them next Friday if possible.

Call 3 You've just heard you have to fly to London next Friday. Call your partner and arrange another time.

MARCH

21 Monday
9 a.m. – 5 p.m. Interviewing candidates for new sales job

22 Tuesday
12–1.30 p.m. Rotary Club lunch

23 Wednesday
9.30 a.m. Marketing conference call
12 noon Lunch with Frank Parker

24 Thursday
9.30 a.m. Take car to garage (no car all day)

25 Friday

▶ COMPLAINTS

1 'The customer is always right.' Do you agree? When you get bad service, who is to blame – the management, the staff, or both?

2 〔3.7〕 Listen to a telephone call between an agent at a car rental company and a customer. What's the customer complaining about?

| **outrageous** shocking, making you very angry | **spot** a particular place |

3 〔3.7〕 Listen again and answer these questions.

a   Why does the customer say, 'At last, a human being!'?
b   Why does she say, 'Are you still there?'
c   Why didn't she talk to anyone when she returned the car?
d   Why couldn't she have kept the car for four days?
e   Why can't she speak to a supervisor?

4 Now study the conversation below. How could this call have had a better outcome? What could the speakers have done differently? Who is at fault here?

A   Hello.
B   At last, a human being!
A   I beg your pardon?
B   I've just spent half an hour trying to get through your automated answering system.
A   Well, that's nothing to do with me, I'm afraid. What do you want?
B   I rented a car from your company in Las Vegas last month. I've just got my credit card bill and I see you've charged me $390. I only had the car for one day so you've made a mistake.
A   What's your name?
B   Eliane Poitier.
A   And you rented the car in …
B   Las Vegas.
A   What date was that?
B   March 7th and you billed American Express on the 14th. … Hello? … Are you still there?
A   Yeah, I'm just looking it up. OK. It says here, you had the car for four days.
B   That's nonsense. I only had it for four hours.

5 〔3.8〕 Now listen to another conversation. Do the speakers do any of the things you suggested? How is the outcome different?

6 〔3.8〕 Listen again and make a note of all the differences with the first conversation. How did they improve the outcome?

7 〔3.9〕 Read this conversation with a partner. Think of ways to make it more courteous, then compare your suggestions with the recording.

A   You've made a mistake on this invoice.
B   Oh yeah?
A   You've charged us for eight pieces but we only received six.
B   The delivery receipt says eight and you signed it.
A   I want to see a copy of that.
B   You want me to fax it to you?

8 〔3.10〕 Do the same thing with this conversation.

A   We're sending these goods back, so we want a refund.
B   Then you must pay a 20% handling fee.
A   Nobody told us that!
B   Read clause five of the contract.
A   Twenty per cent! That's not fair!
B   We always charge that. Tough luck!

✳   See page 72 in the language notes.

A   What price did they give you when you checked the car back in?
B   It was a Sunday so your office shut early. I returned the car to its spot and dropped the keys in the box.
A   So you didn't talk to any of our people?
B   No.
A   Then how do we know you're telling the truth?
B   That's outrageous! I left Las Vegas on the Monday, so I couldn't have kept the car for four days.
A   Can you prove it?
B   I'd like to speak to a supervisor.
A   We don't have supervisors here, I'm afraid. We all work in a team.
B   Well, I'm telling American Express I'm not going to pay this bill.

Task

Work with a partner. One person should look at the information below and the other should look at the information in File 8 on page 59.

You went on a business trip to the UK last month and hired the services of an interpreter for a meeting. You've just received this invoice and it is much higher than it should be. Read your notes and then call the company and complain. Be polite and reasonable.

Eloquencia

Translation and interpreting services

139 Cavendish Street
Tonbridge
Kent TN12 4SP

E: details@eloquenciatrans.
co.uk

T: 01622 743421

Invoice: No. 964325
Order: No. 864/J
Date: 3 March

Office use only

Description		Unit price	Total
Interpreting services	*The meeting was only 8 hours.* 12 hours @ £100		1,200.00
Translation of a contract	*Asked the interpreter to explain a clause of a contract. She misunderstood and gave me a written translation.*		395.00
Travel expenses		90 miles @ £0.50 a mile	64.00
Meals *I bought her lunch.*	*Drove her to the meeting myself in my car.*		30.00
Express shipping		*What's this?*	80.00
Telephone		*What's this?*	57.00
Materials		*And this?*	45.00
		Sub Total	1,871.00
		What's this? **VAT@17.5%**	327.43
		TOTAL	£2,198.43

Payment terms: 30 days

Indirect questions

Begin these questions: *Could you tell me ...?* or *Do you know ...?*

a   What time do the banks close?
b   Where's the nearest chemist?
c   Does this bus go to Terminal 4?
d   What time does the restaurant open?
e   How do I get to the city centre from here?
f   Is there an Internet café near here?

✳   See page 72 in the language notes.

▶ GOING PLACES

Play this game with a partner. You're competitors racing to meet a customer in Beijing. One person starts in New York and the other in London. The first one to get there is the winner.

> **Toss a coin to move.**
> Heads – move one square.
> Tails – move two squares.
>
> **Follow the instructions in each place you visit.**
> **Good luck!**

9 Sydney
You'd like to hire a car for a day or two to see around. Phone a rental company, check the costs for mileage, insurance, etc., and book one if the price is OK.

1 New York
You've only got one day to spend in New York. Ask another passenger to recommend some things to do.

8 Auckland
You're having a quiet night in. Call hotel housekeeping and ask for more towels. Then call room service and order a meal. Fly direct to Singapore.

10 Singapore
Someone asks how late pubs and bars stay open in your country. Explain the laws and customs regarding the sale of alcohol.

2 Washington
Your cell phone should work all over the world, but it won't work here. Call the telephone company and complain.

11 Taipei
Call your boss. Give them an update on your trip's progress so far. Tell them when you will be back.

3 Miami
You can't find your credit card. You think perhaps you lost it at the beach. Call the credit card company.

7 Honolulu
Invite another traveller for a meal tonight. Find out what sort of food they like and fix a time and place to meet.

12 Tokyo
The music from the hotel's karaoke bar is keeping you awake at night. Complain to the hotel manager.

4 Mexico City
You left the power cable for your lap top computer in the last hotel you stayed in. Call and see if they've found it and arrange for them to send it on.

6 Buenos Aires
You've woken up with a bad toothache. Call the dentist and get an appointment as soon as possible. Go back to Mexico City.

13 Beijing
You've made it! Congratulations! Invite everybody to come out and celebrate with you tonight.

5 Rio de Janeiro
You want to buy your Chinese customer a present. Ask another passenger to suggest some suitable gifts.

9 Bombay

You've forgotten to bring any samples of your products with you. Call a colleague and ask them to get some shipped to your hotel as soon as possible.

START

10 Bangkok

You're not sure how to greet people. Should you bow or shake hands? Ask another traveller if they know the customs here and other places in the world.

1 London

You've only got one day to spend in London. Ask another passenger to recommend some things to do.

11 Hong Kong

You'd like to have a suit made. Go to the tailor and find out how long it would take and how much it would cost.

8 Moscow

You gave the hotel laundry service your suit to clean. It hasn't come back yet, but they've delivered a bag containing someone else's underwear to your room. Call them.

2 Paris

You bought a disposable camera to take some photos of the Eiffel Tower. It doesn't work. Take it back and get a refund.

12 Seoul

A colleague calls you and asks how your trip's going. Tell them some of the things that have happened to you.

7 Warsaw

Phone your customer in Beijing. Tell them when you will be arriving and confirm your arrangements to meet. The Polish zloty rises by 100%. Buy yourself a first class ticket and fly direct to Bombay.

3 Madrid

You need to get some documents translated into Chinese. Call a translation agency and check their prices. If they're OK, make the necessary arrangements.

13 Beijing

You've made it! Congratulations! Invite everybody to come out and celebrate with you tonight.

6 Munich

You're not feeling well. Tell the doctor what's wrong with you. Go back to Rome.

5 Zurich

Someone asks about driving regulations in your country. Explain the laws regarding age, tests, and alcohol.

4 Rome

See if another traveller would like to eat with you tonight, then phone a restaurant on the Via Veneto and book a table.

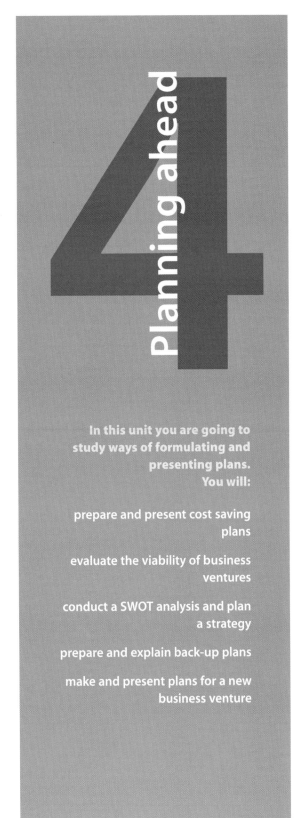

Planning ahead

In this unit you are going to study ways of formulating and presenting plans. You will:

prepare and present cost saving plans

evaluate the viability of business ventures

conduct a SWOT analysis and plan a strategy

prepare and explain back-up plans

make and present plans for a new business venture

> PRESENTING PLANS

1 Name some different sources of power, for example, power from burning fossil fuels like coal and solar power. What sources of energy would you like your government to invest in and why?

2 If there were a proposal to build a wind farm in your neighbourhood, would you object? Why/Why not?

3 `4.1` You're going to hear an electric power station manager talking at a public meeting about some plans to build a wind farm. What questions do you think the local residents will ask him? Listen and find out whether the audience asks the questions you expect.

---

to be **about to** do something to be on the point of doing something very soon
due expected or planned to happen
favourable good, supportive to the plan
a **landscape** the appearance of an area

a **range** a variety or selection of things that belong to the same group
a **turbine** a motor driven by a wheel turned by water, wind, or gas
to **upgrade** to improve or raise the standard of something
visible can be seen or noticed

4 4.1 Listen again and decide if these statements are true or false. Correct those that are wrong.

a They're going to build the wind farm very soon.

b They expect the results of the wind tests on Rider's Hill to be good.

c They want to build at least twenty-two turbines.

d The turbines won't be visible from Logan Road.

e They're going to upgrade an existing farm road to get access to the site.

f They want to reduce their fossil fuel consumption by 20% over the next four years.

g They think they can produce enough electricity for around 8,000 homes.

h They haven't decided what type of turbine to use yet.

5 4.1 Listen again and make a list of all the different verbs and expressions the people used to express their thoughts about the future. Find verbs that express:

a their feelings about the future, e.g. *want*

b their intentions, e.g. *plan*

c how certain they feel, e.g. *doubt*.

What expressions do they use to indicate when something will happen?

(✱) See pages 70–71 in the language notes.

6 What work do you have planned for the future? Are you engaged in any projects or do you have any special tasks on your agenda?

Work with a partner and take it in turns to explain your plans. Use as many different future verbs and expressions as you can.

Task

1 Your company needs to reduce its energy bills and you're responsible for planning how to do it. Brainstorm ideas for reducing energy consumption. Think of as many different ideas as you can.

2 Choose the ideas you like most and prepare to present them to your management. Consider these questions.

– Exactly what needs to be done?

– Will you do it yourselves or employ someone else to do it? (Who?)

Also make some rough estimates for:

– how long it will take

– how much investment is needed

– what the savings will be.

3 Present your plans to the class. Question each other closely and find out who has the best ideas.

▶ PREDICTIONS

1 Is your PC important to your work? How have upgrades in hardware and software changed the way you work? What things can you do more quickly and easily now than you did a few years ago?

2 Read these statements. Do you agree with them? Look at the words in *italics*. Can you suggest words you could substitute and still say the same thing?

a   PCs *are definitely going to* get more powerful in the future.
b   People *are likely to* stop writing on keyboards and talk to their computers instead.
c   We *might* have PCs that turn on instantly, so we won't have to wait for them to come to life.
d   PCs *probably won't* become more reliable. We can expect them to keep crashing.
e   PCs will always be user-unfriendly. They *certainly aren't going to* get simpler to use.

3 Insert these alternative expressions in the correct sentence in 2 above.

could	definitely won't	aren't likely to
will certainly	are probably going to	

（✳） See pages 70–71 in the language notes.

4 How do you think advances in technology will affect your work in the future? Look at these future predictions. How likely do you think they are to happen? Change each one by inserting a phrase that shows how certain you feel.
e.g. *The work I do **isn't likely to** be done by computers.*

When you've finished, compare your opinions with a partner.

a   The work you do is going to be performed by computers.
b   Your company's going to do more business on the Worldwide Web.
c   The Internet will get smaller.

d   In three years the most common language on the Internet is going to be Chinese.
e   You'll work from home, rather than going to an office in another place.
f   Governments will track their citizens' movements using data collected from credit cards, cash machines, video cameras, etc.
g   Teachers and trainers are going to be replaced by computers.
h   Computers will translate what we say into different languages.

Task

1 You're going to play an investment game. You can play alone or in teams. Each individual or team has a portfolio with 100 shares in each of the companies opposite. All shares are currently valued at $100. Read about the companies. Which shares are most likely to increase in value and why?

2 Now it's time to trade. There's no money in this game, but you can exchange or swap shares with other players. For example, you can exchange 10 shares in one company for 15 or 20 shares in another. Decide which shares to trade and negotiate deals with another player or team. Everyone must make at least one trade. Try to improve your portfolios, and make a note of your deals opposite.

3 〔4.2〕 Listen to the radio business news. Discuss which shares are likely to increase in value, which are likely to fall, and why.

4 It's time to trade again. Negotiate deals with another player or team. You can trade as many shares as you want, but everyone must make at least one more trade. Try to improve your portfolio and make a note of your deals.

5 〔4.3〕 Listen to the stock market report and note down the share prices for the four companies. Work out how much your shares are worth. The winner of the game is the person or team with the most valuable portfolio.

Company information	Start with	Position after trade 1	Position after trade 2	Final share value
Connect-X (computer components) This computer component manufacturer makes graphics cards, modem cards, sound cards, and hard disk controllers. It has just developed a technology that uses light waves to make super-fast connections inside PCs. PCs built with its components can run fifteen times faster than standard PCs.	100 shares			
H2 (electric automobiles) This automobile company has been developing an electric car that runs on water, burning hydrogen gas. The company says the car can accelerate from 0 to 80 km/h in 8 seconds and travel 480 kilometres before it runs out of water. It plans to launch the car next spring.	100 shares			
Virtware (virtual pets) This software company has created virtual pets to sell over the web. Customers can buy and download dogs, cats, horses, and even fantastic little animals from outer space. The pets live in a virtual world on a computer's hard drive. In market tests, Virtware pet owners have become obsessed with their cyber animals.	100 shares			
Empraxo (pharmaceuticals) This global pharmaceutical company is currently performing clinical trials for its new drug, Zumoxin. The trials are not yet completed, but the results so far indicate that Zumoxin can cure certain types of cancer, including some common forms of lung and breast cancer.	100 shares			

to **accelerate** to go faster
to **close at** to finish the day's trading on the stock market at a certain price
to **file for bankruptcy** to send an official document to a court of law saying that you do not have enough money to pay your debts

inaccessible not possible to be reached or entered
injured hurt; harmed
an **injury lawsuit** a legal argument in a court of law where one person wants money from another because the other person injured them

to be **obsessed** to have your mind filled with something all the time
a **portfolio** a collection of investments owned by a person or group
to **run out of** something to finish your supply of something

a **side effect** an unpleasant effect something may have in addition to the effects it is expected to have
top-traded traded the most

▶ STRATEGY

1 Which of the following strategies do you think your company should follow and why?

a Should it focus its energies on its largest and most profitable customers or its smallest, least profitable ones?

b Should it try to upgrade or downgrade its services and products?

c Should it aim to develop products/services with high or low margins?

2 Work with a partner. One person should read the case study below and the other should read the one in File 12 on page 60.

In the mid-1960s, a new technology developed in the steel industry. 'Minimill' technology didn't look very important at the time because it could only produce low-quality steel but it had a cost advantage. It was 15% cheaper than the traditional large-scale steel-making processes.

The well-established big steel companies knew their most profitable customers wanted top-quality steel so they invested in upgrading their products. The low-end customers were an insignificant, low-margin segment of the market and the big steel mills were almost relieved to lose them. Investors approved of this strategy and the share prices of the big steel companies rose. So the big manufacturers didn't want to move down-market, but their minimill competitors wanted to move up. The new technology advanced and minimill producers now control over 50% of the total steel market. Big steel manufacturers have to operate in a price-competitive industry where their large-scale production technology is a disadvantage.

3 Compare the two cases. Ask and answer these questions with your partner.

a What new technology were your cases about and when were they developed?

b What was the old or established technology?

c Why didn't the new technologies look important at the beginning?

d What strategy did the established companies in the markets follow?

e Did their investors agree with them?

f What happened to the established companies in the end?

4 Do these adjectives usually convey a positive or negative meaning?

a low-end   e down-market
b viable   f large-scale
c dynamic   g fast-growth
d insignificant   h high-margin

Which of these adjectives are connected with: money, speed, quality, and size?

5 Look at the adjectives in these expressions. What are the opposites?

a a high-margin product
b large-scale production
c a fast-growth industry
d a well-managed company
e a low-end customer
f a down-market product
g top-quality steel
h ever-increasing costs

insignificant small and not important
low-end bottom of a range
a **margin** the amount of profit that a company makes on something

to **move down-market** to shift focus to cheaper and lower-quality products
relieved pleased because your worry has been taken away
a **segment** a section or part of something

6 What do you think the established steel-makers and mini-computer companies should have done? Could they have stopped minimills and PCs taking market share?

Read this Harvard professor's opinion and see if you agree with him.

7 Can you think of any more examples of disruptive technologies? Is your company under threat from anything like this? Can you suggest any solutions to the dilemma? When you have finished turn to File 16 on page 62 and find out what Professor Clayton Christensen suggests.

According to Professor Clayton Christensen, the PC and minimill are both examples of a disruptive technology. Disruptive technologies do jobs worse than established technologies, but they are also cheaper, and they can improve over time. So when they do the job adequately, they drive the established technology out of the market.

'It makes sense for an organization to focus on its best customers, and if organizations don't do that, they're going to lose fast to their competition,' says Christensen.

'But companies face a dilemma when disruptive technologies come into their market at the bottom: if they don't focus all their energy on existing customers and upgrading their product line, they'll fail. But if they don't develop the disruptive technology, they'll fail too. And it's just impossible to do both.'

adequately enough for what's needed	**disruptive** causing disturbance

Task

1 Prepare to conduct a SWOT analysis. First decide whether to analyse: your company as a whole, your department, your division, your team, or one of the products or services you provide. Then use this chart to make brief notes.

2 Work in small groups and take it in turns to present your SWOT analyses. Listen carefully to each person or group that talks. Discuss how they can make the most of the opportunities and what they can do about the threats.

S *trengths*
The things you're good at. The advantages you have over the competition, such as a good geographic position, dynamic employees, etc.
....
....

W *eaknesses*
The things you do poorly compared to your rivals. The disadvantages you have, such as lack of resources, skills, or technologies.
....
....

O *pportunities*
Things that are happening outside the company that could lead to improved results in the future. For example, political changes that could result in increases in demand, new markets, etc.
....
....

T *hreats*
Things that are happening outside the company that could lead to worse results in the future. For example, economic changes that could bring reductions in demand, government restrictions, etc.
....
....

▶ BACK-UP PLANS

1 What projects take place in your company? Do you ever have problems with projects falling behind schedule or going over budget and why?

2 [4.4] A company is setting up a website and here's the budget for the project. Listen to the project manager discussing it with a colleague. What changes does he anticipate? Make alterations to the figures.

Design work	$70,000
Content development	$250,000
Graphics development	$50,000
Technical implementation	$300,000

to **blow a budget** to overspend by a large amount	**on track** to have done the amount that was planned
a **demo** showing how something works, short for *demonstration*	a **server** a computer that controls information which can be shared by a group of connected computers
a **hit** a visit to a website	
in case because something might happen	to **set** someone or something **back** to delay someone or something
the **look and feel** the appearance and interface	

3 [4.4] Listen again and decide whether these statements are true or false. Correct those that are wrong.

a The project is currently on budget.
b The project is currently behind schedule.
c Management originally wanted a simple design that runs fast.
d Management have seen the design and they want something more exciting.
e If management decide to change the look and feel, it will disrupt the schedule.
f The project manager will prepare revised budget figures, if management ask to see them.
g If more people visit the website than expected, the servers will explode.

4 [4.4] Here's an update that the project manager e-mailed to a member of his team. Complete the missing words then listen again to check your answers.

⇦	⇨	✉	✉	⌂	🗑	📎 ▼
Previous	Next	Reply	Reply All	Forward	Delete	Attachments

To:	Jeffries, Fiona
From:	Delaney, Edward
Subject:	Possible changes to website project

It's a tight ¹ .... and we're all under a lot of ² .... , but the good news is everything's on ³ .... However, I should warn you that ⁴ .... management see the design, I think they'll want to change it. The technical implementation won't be affected, ⁵ .... the site gets more hits than we planned, but we may need to change the look and feel. We won't know ⁶ .... management see the demo tomorrow, but I'm getting a revised budget ready now ⁷ .... we do need to make changes.

Eddy

5 What verbs do we often use with these nouns? List as many as you can for each noun.

e.g. to **meet** a deadline

a   a deadline   b   pressure   c   (a) schedule

6 Match these lists to one of the words in 5.

1   to be under, to work under, to feel a lot of, to cope with, to apply, to withstand
2   to keep to, to fall behind, to be on, to stay on, to get ahead of, to draw up, to follow, to disrupt
3   to beat, to be up against, to miss, to work towards, to set

(✳)   See page 73 in the language notes.

QUICK CHECK

Budgets and schedules

1   What's the difference between being:
   a   *on time* and *in time*?
   b   *on budget* and *within budget*?

2   What's the opposite of:
   a   getting ahead of schedule?
   b   overspending?
   c   doubling a budget?

3   What verbs do we often use with the word *money*? List as many as you can.

   e.g. to *spend money*, to *save money*
   How many of these verbs can you use with the word *time* as well?

---

7 Look at the words in *italics* below. If you replace them with *if*, how does the meaning of the sentence change?

a   *When* they see the design, they'll want to change it.
   (How certain is it that they will see the design?)

b   She won't alter the budget, *unless* they tell her to.
   (Will she obey instructions?)
c   She'll draw up a new budget *in case* they want to make changes.
   (Will she draw it up now or later?)
d   She won't implement the changes *until* they tell her to.
   (Will she implement the changes and if so, when?)

(✳)   See pages 71–72 in the language notes.

8 Use the phrases below to make some sentences about yourself.

a   I can't go home tonight until …
b   I'm going to retire when …
c   I'm taking out travel insurance in case …
d   I won't get promoted unless …
e   I'll learn English faster if …
f   I'm going to keep on learning English until …
g   I'll get a new car when …
h   I usually carry … around with me, in case …
i   I'll …, if …
j   I'm planning to … next week, unless …

Task

1 What's on your work schedule for the next few weeks? Write a list of the tasks you need to accomplish and explain them to another student.

2 The problems below frequently disrupt schedules. Which ones might disrupt yours? What can you do about it if they do? Think of some back-up plans.

a   Someone's illness or absence
b   Missing items or documentation
c   Equipment breakdowns
d   People changing their minds
e   Other unexpected events (what?)

3 Tell your partner about some things that could disrupt your schedule and explain your back-up plans.

▶ NEW VENTURES

1 Have you ever thought about starting your own business? What gave you the idea? What sort of qualities do you think an entrepreneur needs to be successful?

2 Here's some advice for entrepreneurs. Read it and discuss these questions.

a Which points are most important and why?
b Can you suggest any other things that are important?

Now read the interview below and find out if Fred Abrew would agree with you.

Advice for entrepreneurs

Work 7 days a week and 18 hours a day.

Treat your employees well.

Buy low, sell high, pay late, and collect early.

Listen carefully to your customers.

Do what you believe in and love what you do.

Use your contacts – network, network, network.

Learn from your mistakes and act quickly.

Look for wealthy venture capitalists.

When Fred Abrew retired as President and CEO of Equitable Resources Inc, a public utility company, he said goodbye to lunches at his club, the corporate jet, and a secretary to screen his calls. But instead of relaxing somewhere on a beach, Fred is working harder than ever building EnergyE-comm.com, an Internet startup that provides e-business services and software tools to energy companies. So, wondering what it takes to become a successful Internet entrepreneur, we asked Fred:

What inspired you to start your own business?

I had a belief in the potential of technology. I looked at the industry I worked in and I saw a lot of the executives were marking time because they didn't understand what technology could do. It was a problem for the industry, but an opportunity for me.

What sort of qualities do you think an entrepreneur needs to be successful?

You have to believe that you're doing something valuable and you have to work very hard and stick at it. You need lots of energy.

If someone was setting up an Internet startup, what advice would you give them?

Try to gain brand recognition. At EnergyE-comm.com we wanted to get our name known as the energy industry's expert on e-commerce, so we evaluated different energy companies' websites and compared their performance. They wanted to read the results, so it's spread our name and

helped to create our market place. You've got to get a market place and then you've got to listen very carefully to your customers to get ideas and information.

Do things happen faster in startups than large companies?

Oh yes. If you're trying to innovate and do new things, you're going to have some failures. If something's wrong, you've got to spot it fast, learn from it and then re-do a lot of things very quickly.

What new skills have you needed to develop?

I had to go up a huge learning curve to understand the technology. But in a way, running a startup is like running any other business, and I understood what it took when I started.
I don't have the perks and support I used to have when I was an executive in a large company any more. But I've always enjoyed doing things rather than having things done for me, so I'm having a ball.

---

brand recognition a situation where people know the name of a product or service

to **have a ball** enjoy yourself and have a very good time
a **learning curve** a period when you learn a lot very fast

to **mark time** to pass time doing routine and uninteresting things
a **startup** a new company

to **stick at something** continue to do something even though it's difficult
what it takes what something needs or requires

3 Answer these questions with a partner.

a What did Fred Abrew do before he founded EnergyE-comm.com?

b What does EnergyE-comm.com do?

c How did he get the idea for the company?

d How did EnergyE-comm.com gain brand recognition?

e What do you think the major challenge has been at EnergyE-comm.com?

4 You have decided to follow Fred's example and start your own new business. Find some other students who you'd like to set up in business with and form a team. You have lots of decisions to make about the new venture. Discuss these questions with your fellow entrepreneurs.

1 What sort of company are you going to set up? Products? (What?) Services? (What?)

2 Who are your potential customers? How large is the market and is it growing?

3 What competition is there? How will your product/service be different from others on the market? How will it be unique or special?

4 How will you reach your customers and persuade them to buy from you rather than the competition?
   Where will you advertise? What image are you looking for? How will you promote your product/service?

5 What will the company's legal status be? (Partnership, limited liability, charity, co-operative, publicly-owned, etc.)
   Who will own the equity? Who will be on the management team? What relevant experience and knowledge do they have?

6 What staff will you need?
   What will you be looking for when you select them? (Educational background, experience, attitudes, etc.)
   How will you train and motivate them?

7 What are the biggest risks you face and how will you overcome them? What significant opportunities do you have and how will you take advantage of them?

5 Prepare to present your business plan to a group of venture capitalists. Decide what you need to tell them and which member of your team will talk about what.

6 Take it in turns to play the roles of the venture capitalists and the entrepreneurs. Each team of entrepreneurs presents their business plan and answers questions from the venture capitalists. When you have finished, take a vote on which team had the best business idea.

8 How much capital will you need to start the company? What budgets will you need? (For equipment, staff, overheads, etc.)
   How much of the equity are you willing to exchange in return for finance? (Are you prepared to surrender control if necessary?)

In this unit you are going to study ways of resolving conflict through negotiation and awareness of cultural differences. You will:

identify and drop hints

consider alternative options and their consequences

negotiate solutions to business problems

resolve cultural conflicts in an international meeting

reach an agreement on a global standardization issue

▶ DROPPING HINTS

1 ⌈5.1⌋ Sometimes people don't say what they mean.

Listen to people saying these things:

a   What do you think they really mean?
b   How would you reply?

1   Those chocolates look nice.
2   You said you'd be here by eight.
3   Are you busy?
4   Is anybody else here feeling hot?
5   Goodness, is that the time?
6   Is that your car in my parking space?
7   I thought I put a cup of coffee down here.
8   You should have been with **us** last night!
9   I liked most parts of your proposal.

2 Now match these replies to a comment above.

a   Yes, I got held up.
b   Well, **I** haven't taken it.
c   Please help yourself.
d   So what didn't you like?
e   Why, what happened?
f   Why, will it take long?
g   I'm afraid the air conditioning's not working.
h   Oh sorry. I'll move it.
i   Yes, do you have to go?

3 ⟦5.2⟧ Listen to some people arranging a schedule for a company visit. How direct do you think they are? Number these items in the order they will happen.

- ☐ Review of the sales figures
- ☐ Meeting with Knut Fliedner
- ☐ Meeting with Laura Berne
- ☐ Introduction to the team
- ☐ Meeting with Julio Ramon
- ☐ Lunch at a nearby restaurant

4 Do you think the woman was happy with the schedule? Why/Why not?

5 ⟦5.3⟧ Listen to her discussing what happened with a colleague and make a note of the things she doesn't like about the schedule.

6 ⟦5.2⟧ Listen to the first dialogue again. How exactly did the woman indicate that she wasn't happy with the schedule? Who do you think was at fault here; the woman for being too indirect or the man for not listening?

7 Do people in your culture tend to say what they want directly or do they drop hints? Do you know of other cultures in other parts of the world that are more/less direct?

Task

1 Work with a partner. You're going to negotiate the schedule for a company visit. The host should use the information in File 13 on page 61 and the visitor should turn to File 1 on page 56 .

2 When you've finished, compare your notes with your partner. Were you aware of all the things they wanted? Do you think you achieved a good compromise on all the points?

QUICK CHECK

British and American English

1 What's this date in American English and what is it in British English?
6/7/2002

2 Look at the words in *italics*. Would an American (A) or British (B) person say these things? What would people say on the opposite side of the Atlantic? Check your answers below.

a He made a *collect* call.
b I *rang* his *mobile* but it was *engaged*.
c Our *wage bills* rose by 20% last year.
d Our office is open Monday *through* Friday from a quarter *of* nine to five thirty, but we're closed *on* weekends.
e I'm on *holiday* for the next *fortnight*.
f See you next *fall*.
g I'd like a *return* ticket, please.

3 If an American says these things, what do they probably mean? And what about if a British person says them?

a How are you doing?
b Our turnover increased by 4%.
c Are you mad?
d Can we have our check/cheque?

Answers

1 US: June 7th; UK: 6th July

2 a A – reverse charge, b B – called, cell phone, busy c B – labor costs, d A – to, at, e B – vacation, two weeks, f A – autumn, g B – round trip

3 a How are you?/What progress are you making? b staff turnover/ income or gross revenues c angry/crazy d We want the bill/We want payment

▶ CAREER DILEMMAS

1 What is the most difficult career decision you've ever made? Why was it hard?

QUICK CHECK

'Problem' vocabulary

Match a word on the left to an example on the right.

a   a problem
b   an issue
c   a dilemma
d   a paradox
e   a suggestion
f   a solution

1   Why don't you change jobs?
2   Job satisfaction.
3   Find a new job.
4   I'm bored with my job.
5   Shall I change jobs or not?
6   Many people have boring jobs, yet still enjoy their work.

2 [5.4] Listen to someone talking about their career. What dilemma are they facing? Imagine you were in this situation. What would you do?

It'd depend on ...
I'd need to know/consider ...
If they paid me more, I'd take the job.

3 Now read what an American executive did when he was faced with a similar dilemma and answer these questions.

a   Did he do what you'd have done?
b   Why did he accept the job?
c   Why does he think he made the right choice?

choked up emotional	to **head up** to lead
to **get to thinking** to begin or start the process of thinking	to **put up with** to tolerate
	to **turn down** to refuse

Richard LeFauve loved his job as President of General Motors Saturn Corporation so when the company asked him to head up a new 'virtual' university he turned the job down three times. But then he got to thinking: 'You're not going to live forever. And what's more, they're not going to put up with you forever.' He realized it was an opportunity to create something that could last long after he was gone. The fourth time GM offered him the job Richard accepted and he has no doubts that he made the right choice. 'I've had people come up to me choked up about what the GM University experience has meant to them personally and professionally,' he says. 'I've heard them use phrases like "life-changing event".'

4 How could this story have turned out differently? What would have happened if Richard had made different decisions?

5 Underline all the verbs in these sentences. What tenses are they?

If Richard hadn't accepted the job, he would have regretted it.
If someone offered me a job like that, I'd accept it.

Both these conditional forms are used to describe imaginary situations, but how are they used differently?

(✳) See page 72 in the language notes.

6 Now consider another dilemma. Follow the same procedure as before.

a 5.5 Listen first and say what you would do in this situation.
b Read what another manager did when he was faced with a similar dilemma. See if you think he made the right choice.
c Say what would have happened if he'd made a different decision.

When Andy Bechtolsheim left Sun Microsystems in 1995 and started his own software company, the future looked promising for his product, Gigabit Ethernet switching. But within a year, the market was filling up with well-financed startups as well as large, established competitors. Bechtolsheim's product had superior technology but he didn't have established sales channels. So in late 1996, he sold out to Cisco, a large player in the software field. He might have made a different choice 15 years ago. 'Then you had slow-moving, traditional companies, and it was easier to compete against them,' he says. 'Now, the window of opportunity has shrunk.' In the end, Bechtolsheim's decision was strictly business. 'I don't claim much intelligence here,' he says. 'I looked at the market, and the choice was clear.'

| **promising** showing signs of being very good or successful | to **shrink** to get smaller |

Task

1 Work with a partner. You're both facing difficult career dilemmas and you need some advice. One person should read role A and the other should read role B. Then close your books and present your problem to your partner. Find out what they would do.

Role A

You've worked loyally for the same company for almost 20 years. Your boss is tough, but you've learnt a lot from him and recently he gave you a challenging assignment – a marketing project. You've been putting a lot of effort into it and you know you're doing it right. But your boss doesn't think so and yesterday, in a meeting in front of all your colleagues, he put down all your hard work. He made you look small and it was very embarrassing. It's clear that your efforts are not appreciated and you're very angry about it. In fact, you're wondering whether to quit.

Role B

You own a small marketing company that you founded three years ago. Business is good and you know you're going to be making a lot of money in three or four years. But it's not easy at the moment. You're chasing new customers, working long hours, and you need more capital, which you can only get by investing more of your personal funds. One of your major clients has offered you a job. The salary's generous, but you're not sure whether you want to stop being the boss and become a company employee again.

capital an amount of money you invest in a new business	to **put down** to say something to make someone
to **chase** to run after something	seem foolish or stupid
funds available money	to **quit** to leave a job (informal)

2 It's now two years later and things have moved on. Find out what happened to you. A should read the information in File 5 on page 58 and B should read the information in File 11 on page 60.

▶ NEGOTIATING

1 What is a negotiation? Is it:

a a discussion between people with conflicting interests in order to reach an agreement?

b an opportunity to form new or better business alliances?

c one of the difficult conversations we all have every day. Life is a negotiation?

2 ⟨5.6⟩ A European bicycle manufacturer wants to break into the US market. Two managers from the company are preparing for a negotiation with a potential distributor. Listen and answer these questions.

a How many bicycles do they hope the distributor can sell?

b What do they need to work out?

c What's the main problem they expect to have in the negotiation?

d Would a two- or three-year contract be good or bad?

e What alternative do they have if they can't come to an agreement?

3 ⟨5.6⟩ Try to remember the missing words in these sentences, then listen again and check your answers.

a I intend .... them that question.

b We can offer .... the discount if they sell more.

c Yes, we need .... a sliding scale.

d We should avoid .... any long-term agreements like that.

e I can't help .... we might be better off saying 'no' to these people.

f We can keep .... There are other distributors.

g But we can't afford .... too long.

✱ See page 74 in the language notes.

4 ⟨5.7⟩ Now listen to the negotiation and answer these questions.

a What exactly does the distributor want?

b Why does the manufacturer say, 'Well that changes things a little'?

| to **carve a market niche** to create a place that is yours in a section of a market, often through hard work | an **option** an alternative |
| **exclusive** not to be shared, just for you | a **sliding scale** a chart that makes one quantity dependent on another, so they increase or decrease together |

5 Do you think the manufacturer should accept the distributor's terms? Why/Why not? Complete this e-mail with an infinitive (*to do*) or gerund (*doing*) form of the verbs in brackets as in the examples. Do you agree with the writer?

```
┌─────────────────────────────────────┐
│ □                              回回 │
│ ⇦      ⇨     ᐦ     ᐦ    ᐦ   🗑   📎 ▾ │
│ Previous Next Reply Reply All Forward Delete Attachments │
│ ┌─────┬────────────────────────────┐▲│
│ │To:  │ Wade, Rob                  │ │
│ │From:│ Mullins, Jackie            │ │
│ │Subject:│ The US distribution deal│▼│
│ └─────┴────────────────────────────┘ │
│ ┌──────────────────────────────────┐▲│
│ │I can't help thinking (think) this is a poor offer│
│ │and I'd advise you to reject (reject) it, or at least│
│ │postpone ¹ .............. (sign) the agreement until│
│ │we've had a chance to talk.        │
```

I can't help <u>thinking</u> (think) this is a poor offer and I'd advise you <u>to reject</u> (reject) it, or at least postpone [1] .... (sign) the agreement until we've had a chance to talk.

The sales promised by the distributor are very high, but I think that's because they intend [2] .... (sell) our bicycles at discount prices. If we allow them [3] .... (do) this, we risk [4] .... (damage) both our margins and our image. We've managed [5] .... (carve) a high-end niche in our home market, and while it's very tempting [6] .... (go) for the volume sales here, we should avoid [7] .... (do) anything that could damage our reputation in our home market.

I think we should go on [8] .... (look) for alternative distributors and, if not, consider [9] .... (set up) our own sales organization in the US.

6 Below are some negotiating phrases from the conversation. Which ones:

a   encourage people to talk?
b   say what you want?
c   show you're listening?

1   We need to ...
2   Going back to the point you made about ...
3   Would you like to start things off?
4   You mentioned ... and I wonder ...
5   Tell me more.
6   We'd prefer to ...
7   So you're saying ...?
8   We'd like to ...
9   Please go on.

Task

1   Here are some business problems where an agreement has to be negotiated. Read them and decide which ones you would like to act out. Decide who will play each side and split into two negotiating teams.

2   Before you start the negotiation, discuss these questions with your negotiating team.

a   What exactly do you want from this negotiation?
b   What do you think the other side will want?
c   What do you think the main areas of disagreement will be?

3   Meet with the other side and exchange your proposals. Try to negotiate an agreement that everyone feels happy about.

a In order to reduce travel costs, a petroleum company gets its employees to take the cheapest available flights when they travel on business. This means they often have to fly inconvenient routes and make long stopovers and they say it's damaging their ability to perform effectively.

b A pharmaceutical company contracted a marketing agency to plan the launch of a new drug. But the drug failed to get government approval and was scrapped. The contract says the marketing agency is entitled to 100% of the fee, although they only did 20% of the work. The pharmaceutical company does not want to pay the full fee.

c A bank has a customer support team that deals with client account inquiries and transactions over the phone. The marketing division of the bank wants the customer support team to ask clients questions when they call and complete a five-page questionnaire to gather marketing data. The support staff say it will take too long, they don't have time and the customers won't like it.

to **gather** to collect
inconvenient causing difficulty or problems
a **launch** the introduction of a new product to a market

to **scrap** to dispose of something that you don't want any more
a **stopover** a short stop between parts of a long journey

▶ GOING GLOBAL

1 Choose the answer you agree with most.

a Business is about:
- ☐ making money.
- ☐ having fun.

b Managers should:
- ☐ listen to workers then make the decisions.
- ☐ advise, but let workers make the decisions.

c Employees with specialist skills are:
- ☐ valuable.
- ☐ a liability.

2 Read this article on AES, a multinational power generation company. Would AES agree with your answers in 1 above?

to **dumb down** to make stupid; reduce the level of knowledge it requires to understand something a **front-line worker** worker engaged in performing the tasks rather than managing **fulfilling** satisfying your hopes and dreams	**mundane** ordinary, not interesting or exciting the **root** the cause or source of something **talented** showing natural skill or ability **well-rounded** having a wide range of knowledge and abilities

3 Discuss these questions with a partner.

a Should it be a company's responsibility to ensure work is 'fun, fulfilling and exciting'?

b How sensible is it to give large responsibilities to young employees straight from college?

c Do you think that having specialists around dumbs down an organization?

d Who should have the ultimate power in making decisions: management or workers?

e If your company wanted to adopt AES's style of management, what difficulties might it cause? Would you like to work for a company with AES's business values?

4 Study the words *bored* and *boring* in these sentences.

a I'd soon feel *bored* if I had to perform the same mundane tasks all the time.

b Power plant work is often hard, dull, and *boring*.

Boring and *bored* are both adjectives. Which one describes:

1 a quality something has?

2 a reaction to something else?

(✳) See page 74 in the language notes.

IF IT'S NOT FUN, DON'T DO IT

The AES mission statement says that work should be 'fun, fulfilling and exciting'. Dennis Bakke and Richard Sant, the company founders, have picked a tough business in which to have fun. Power-plant work is hard and dangerous. Employees tend to get trained in highly specialized and mundane tasks and end up feeling bored and demotivated. But not at AES. 'Specialization is the root of a lot of boredom,' explains co-founder Bakke. Even worse, he argues, talented specialists tend to dumb down the rest of the organization: 'As soon as you have a specialist who's very good, everyone else quits thinking. The better that person is, the worse it is for the organization. It's well-rounded people who deliver extraordinary performance.' So young AES employees, sometimes straight out of college, have quickly found themselves performing a wide range of challenging tasks, from developing plans for new plants to negotiating contracts.

The best way to exercise power, the AES founders argue, is to give it up. 'The modern manager is supposed to ask his people for advice and then make a decision,' says Bakke. 'But at AES, each decision is made by a person and a team. Their job is to get advice from me and from anybody else they think it's necessary to get advice from. And then they make the decision.' Sant points out: 'If Dennis and I had to lead everything, we couldn't have grown as much as we have.'

5 Select the correct adjective in *italics* in the passage below.

The power plant where I work has recently been taken over by an American company, and it's led to some very ¹ *interested/interesting* changes. I'm ² *amazed/amazing* at the way the place is managed now. The operators are making a lot more of the decisions and their jobs are certainly less ³ *bored/boring* and more ⁴ *fulfilled/fulfilling* as a result. But, some of the managers feel ⁵ *threatened/threatening*. I'm an experienced manager myself and it can be very ⁶ *frustrated/frustrating* to have to stand back and do nothing when you see people making silly mistakes. But I admit I've been pleasantly ⁷ *surprised/surprising* by how few serious mistakes there are. I've seen operators take decisions that I thought were very poor and then been ⁸ *astonished/astonishing* when they worked. But it can be very ⁹ *worried/worrying* for managers like me. If the company isn't ¹⁰ *interested/interesting* in our specialist knowledge and experience, why does it need us?

Task

1 An American company has recently taken over a power plant in your country. A meeting will be held between the parent company and local management from the home country.

There are two items on the agenda for the meeting. Work in pairs or small groups and decide who will represent each party at the meeting. Prepare what to say to argue your case. Then hold the meeting and decide what to do.

1 **A pipe at the plant needs replacing.** A team of operators has been put in charge. The operators are planning to replace the expensive steel pipe with an inexpensive plastic one. The local managers think the plastic pipe will last only a few days and they want to overrule the team. The parent company thinks the operators should decide.

2 **The plant is overstaffed and the workforce must be cut.** The parent company suggests 75% of the workers should be selected for layoffs. The local managers would prefer to introduce a voluntary redundancy programme.

2 Find out what actually happened in a similar situation in Ireland in File 15 on page 62. Did you make the same decisions as the managers made there?

▶ WORKING ACROSS CULTURES

1 Fons Trompenaars, a Dutch social scientist, has conducted research into cultural differences that affect the process of doing business. Here are three questions he asked managers from different countries. Read them with a partner. How would you answer them?

Question 1

What is the best way to improve the quality of life? Should individuals:

a have as much freedom as possible and the maximum opportunity to develop themselves?

b continuously take care of their fellow human beings, even if it obstructs individual freedom and individual development?

Question 2

How do people tend to work in your workplace? Is it:

a as an individual, alone? In this case they are pretty much their own boss. Individuals decide most things themselves and how they get along is their own business. They have to take care of themselves without expecting others to look out for them.

b in a group where everybody works together? Everybody has something to say in the decisions that are made and everybody can count on one another.

Question 3

A mistake has been discovered at work. It was caused by the negligence of one of the members of a team. Who should carry the responsibility for the mistake. Should it be:

a the individual who caused the mistake by their negligence?

b the team that the individual works in?

---

to **count on** someone to rely or depend on someone	**negligence** not being careful enough; lack of care
to **get along** to proceed; to perform	to **obstruct** to stop something from happening or moving
to **look out for** someone to take care of someone's interests	

2 Study Trompenaars' results.

a Which countries seem to have the most individualist culture?

b Which countries tend to be more group-minded?

c Is your country on the chart? If so, do you agree with the results? If not, where do you think your country would rank?

d Do any of the results surprise you?

e How might these differences in attitudes affect the way people do business in different cultures?

Question 1

Percentages of people who thought personal freedom was the best way to improve the quality of life.

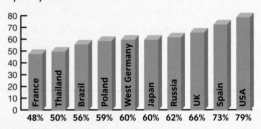

Question 2

Percentages of people who said that people tend to work as individuals in their workplace.

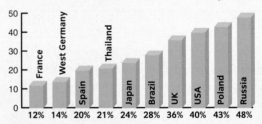

Question 3

Percentages of people who said the individual is responsible for the mistake.

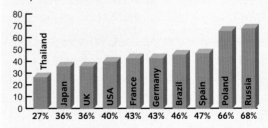

3 Consider the questions below. Say what happens in your culture. How might attitudes be different in other places?

a Do companies usually give rewards to groups or individuals?
b Do managers generally spend a lot of time and effort getting everyone's agreement to a plan before it's implemented?
c Do teams or individuals usually negotiate deals?
d How important is group harmony? Do people feel they should be frank or tactful when someone has made a mistake?

frank saying what you think or feel	**tactful** careful not to say things that could offend people

4 You work for a multinational organization. You have received this e-mail from the Vice President of Global Sales. What do they want you to do and why?

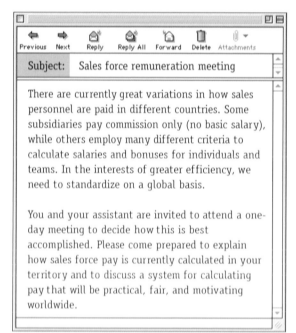

Previous Next Reply Reply All Forward Delete Attachments

Subject: Sales force remuneration meeting

There are currently great variations in how sales personnel are paid in different countries. Some subsidiaries pay commission only (no basic salary), while others employ many different criteria to calculate salaries and bonuses for individuals and teams. In the interests of greater efficiency, we need to standardize on a global basis.

You and your assistant are invited to attend a one-day meeting to decide how this is best accomplished. Please come prepared to explain how sales force pay is currently calculated in your territory and to discuss a system for calculating pay that will be practical, fair, and motivating worldwide.

a **bonus** a payment that is added to what is usual (a) **commission** money paid for selling goods, which goes up with the quantity sold	a **criterion** plural = criteria, the standard you use to make a decision **remuneration** payment

5 Here are different criteria that can be used to calculate pay. Can you think of some more to add to the list? Which ones do you think are most important?

Quantity of sales
Meeting individual or team sales targets
Age
Years of service
Number of dependants
Educational level
Participation in team activities
Level of effort (How can this be measured?)

6 Prepare to hold the meeting. First decide what countries will be represented. (The USA, Thailand, your country, other countries?) Decide who will represent which country and prepare your arguments. Consider:

a how salespeople's salaries are currently calculated in the country you will represent.
b how the salaries should be calculated. What criteria should be used?
c when and how the new salary system should be introduced.

7 Hold the meeting. Try to reach an agreement on a pay structure that everyone thinks is motivating and fair, and which would work on a global basis.

Information files

FILE 1

UNIT 5 Dropping hints task, p47

Here's the schedule you would like for your visit, but you'd rather change it than be impolite. Read it and think about what you can say. Telephone your partner to talk it through. Make alterations where necessary.

9.00 a.m.	You want to avoid the rush hour traffic and start at 10.00 a.m.
10.00 a.m.	Introduction to the marketing team.
11.00 a.m.	Meeting with Axel Meissner. You'd like to meet with Axel before you talk to Mattius.
12.00 a.m.	Meeting with Mattius Andrup.
1.00 p.m.	Lunch. You prefer a late lunch and you're fond of Italian food.
2.00 p.m.	Tour of the new factory site. You don't want to spend too long outside if the weather is cold.
4.00 p.m.	Review of the production targets. You would like to go for a drink with your host after work.

FILE 2

UNIT 2 Great inventions 2, p18

Focus Magazine decided these were mankind's top ten inventions and they ranked them in order of importance. They decided the most important invention was sanitation. Do you agree?

Paragraph	Invention	Ranking
a	Fire	4
b	Transistor	9
c	The wheel	5
d	The Internet	8
e	The printing press	3
f	The laser	10
g	The computer	2
h	Antibiotics	7
i	Sanitation	1
j	The radio	6

FILE 3

UNIT 1 Questioning costs task, p9

You were responsible for producing your company's spring sale brochure. It looks fantastic but the final costs are much higher than your estimates. Your colleague is going to call you about these figures. Read your notes and answer their questions. Invent any information you don't know and try to justify the costs.

Spring sale brochure

Design costs	Budget	Actual	
Labour	£5,300	£6,880	*Management kept making changes.*
Travel expenses	£400	£500	*Extra meetings at the designer's office.*
Photo library charges	£5,000	£5,500	*New photograph for front cover.*

Printing costs	Budget	Actual	
Paper and printing	£2,800	£3,250	*Extra print run – more customers than last year. Price of paper rose.*
Special packaging	£200	£400	*Used stronger packaging.*
Shipping	£300	£395	*Had to keep shipping things to designers.*

TOTAL COSTS	£14,000	£16,925	

FILE 4

UNIT 2 Great inventions 5, p18

This crossword contains some more of mankind's greatest inventions. You have half the words and your partner has the other half. Without naming the inventions, take it in turns to describe the benefits they have brought mankind and help one another complete the crossword. These phrases will help you:

- They enable us to ...
- It allows us to ...
- It's made ... possible.
- It's had a great impact on ...
- It was invented in/by ...
- Before these were invented ...

FILE 5
UNIT 5 Career dilemmas task 2, p49

Read what happened to you and then tell your partner about it. Imagine some of the things that might have happened if you hadn't done what you did.

> In the end you decided that the last thing you wanted to do was make a hasty decision so you cooled off for a few months and evaluated your options. You realized your problems at work involved more than one bad meeting, so you decided to leave the company. The marketing project was a success and shortly before leaving, you received a memo from your boss congratulating you on it. You realized you hadn't wanted to get even with him. You'd just wanted his approval. You've now started your own business and it's going really well.

to **cool off** to calm down	**hasty** quick and without
to **get even with** someone	enough thought
to get revenge	

FILE 6
Unit 2 Great inventions 5, p18

This crossword contains some more of mankind's greatest inventions. You have half the words and your partner has the other half. Without naming the inventions, take it in turns to describe the benefits they have brought mankind and help one another complete the crossword. These phrases will help you:

– They enable us to ...
– It allows us to ...
– It's made ... possible.
– It's had a great impact on ...
– It was invented in/by ...
– Before these were invented ...

FILE 7
UNIT 3 Finding solutions 3, p26

This is what the producer feels he learnt from his experience making *Gorillas in the Mist*.

> 'This experience taught me three things. First, ask high-quality questions, like "What if?" Second, find people who add new perspectives. Third, pay attention to those new voices. As experienced film-makers, we believed that our way was the only way. But the young woman's lack of experience enabled her to see opportunities where we saw only boundaries.'

| a **boundary** a limit; something that stops you from going further | a **perspective** the way you think about something, your point of view |
| to **lack** to have too little or none of something | |

FILE 8

UNIT 3 Complaints task, p33

You own Eloquencia, an interpreting and translation service in the UK. A foreign client hired one of your interpreters last month.

They're going to call about the invoice you've sent them. Read your notes and get ready to explain your charges. Be polite and reasonable.

Eloquencia

Translation and interpreting services

139 Cavendish Street
Tonbridge
Kent TN12 4SP

E: details@eloquenciatrans.
   co.uk

T: 01622 743421

Invoice: No. 964325
Order: No. 864/J
Date: 3 March

Office use only

Description		Unit price	Total
Interpreting services	*8 hours meeting + 2 hours to travel there and 2 hours travel back.*	12 hours @ £100	1,200.00
Translation of contract	*Client asked the interpreter to translate a contract.*		395.00
Travel expenses	*The interpreter is entitled to travel costs (Clause 8 of contract).*	90 miles @ £0.50 a mile	64.00
Meals	*Interpreters working a full day are entitled to claim the cost of lunch (Clause 9 of contract).*		30.00
Express shipping	*Client asked the interpreter to send some papers to their head office.*		80.00
Telephone	*Client used the interpreter's mobile phone to make calls.*		57.00
Materials	*Not sure what this is.*		45.00
		Sub Total	1,871.00
	UK sales tax. **VAT@17.5%**		327.43
Payment terms: 30 days		**TOTAL**	£2,198.43

FILE 9

UNIT 1 Questioning costs task, p9

Your colleague was responsible for producing your company's spring sale brochure. It looks fantastic but the final costs are much higher than the estimates. Study the figures and then call your colleague. Question them closely about all the items and decide whether they were necessary costs.

Spring sale brochure

Design costs	Budget	Actual
Labour	£5,300	£6,880
Travel expenses	£400	£500
Photo library charges	£5,000	£5,500

Printing costs	Budget	Actual
Paper and printing	£2,800	£3,250
Special packaging	£200	£400
Shipping	£300	£395

	Budget	Actual
TOTAL COSTS	£14,000	£16,925

FILE 10

UNIT 3 Reporting problems task, p25

Call 1 Your colleague is currently visiting the UK on business. They call you with a problem. Find out as much as you can about it and promise to look into it.

Call 2 You've spoken to your IT department. They installed new security software onto the system this morning. Your colleague should have received a new password by e-mail. They're going to send it again. Call your colleague.

FILE 11

UNIT 5 Career dilemmas task 2, p49

Read what happened to you and then tell your partner about it. Imagine some of the things that might have happened if you hadn't done what you did.

It was a difficult decision but the salary you were offered was big enough to make you reassess. Your company's future was promising, but you needed more money for additional equipment and staff, which meant you would have had to mortgage your house. You were spending nights worrying about finding new clients and you rarely got home until after your two young children were asleep. So you accepted the offer and you have no regrets. Spending time with your family was more important than being the boss, and now you have the opportunity to do good work without the administrative headaches.

a **headache** something that causes worry or difficulty
to **mortgage** to use property, for example, a house, as security for a loan
to **reassess** to calculate again; to rethink

FILE 12

UNIT 4 Strategy 2, p40

PCs

When PCs were developed in the 1980s, they seemed like toys. They were mostly purchased by individuals who used them to play games, and they were much cheaper than the 'minicomputers' that many medium and large-scale companies used at that time.

The minicomputer industry was very successful. It had dynamic, fast-growth, high-margin companies that investors regarded as some of the best-managed companies in the world. They invested in developing new high-performance, high-margin products that provided customers with ever-increasing computing power.

But PC technology advanced rapidly and businesses replaced their minicomputers with networks of PCs. Several minicomputer makers went out of business and the rest were badly damaged. They couldn't establish a viable position in the new market.

dynamic active; full of energy and ideas
margin the amount of profit that a company makes on something
rapidly very quickly
to **regard** to think of somebody or something (in the way mentioned)
viable will be successful; will work

FILE 13

UNIT 5 Dropping hints task, p47

Here's the schedule you would like for your partner's visit, but you'd rather change it than be impolite. Read it and think about what you can say. Your partner is going to telephone you to talk it through. Make alterations where necessary.

9.00 a.m.	Introduction to the marketing team. You want to make an early start so you can end the visit by 4 p.m.
10.00 a.m.	Tour of the new factory site. The new factory site is about a twenty-minute drive from your office.
12.00 a.m.	Lunch at a Chinese restaurant. There's a nice Chinese restaurant on the way back to the office.
1.00 p.m.	Meeting with Helena da Silva and Mattius Andrup.
2.00 p.m.	Review of the sales targets. Your sales targets are too high and you want them reduced.
3.00 p.m.	Meeting with Axel Meissner. Axel Meissner asked you to schedule this meeting for the afternoon if possible.
4.00 p.m.	You have private work you want to finish before you go home.

FILE 14

UNIT 3 Changing plans task, p31

Call 1 You work for ACI Robotics – a robot manufacturer. Someone calls you when you are away from your desk. Deliver a voicemail message asking them to leave a message after the beep.

Call 2 Return your partner's call. Invite them to take a tour of your manufacturing facilities, offer to arrange a demonstration of your robots in action and arrange a time. Here's your diary for next week.

MARCH

21 Monday

22 Tuesday
9 a.m. Management Now magazine interview
3.30 p.m. Delta project progress meeting

23 Wednesday
2 p.m. Sales presentation at Turbolink Inc.

24 Thursday

25 Friday

26 Saturday	27 Sunday

Call 3 Your partner calls with a problem. Try to help.

FILE 15

UNIT 5 Going global task, p53

TURNING OVER POWER

In 1992, AES teamed up with a Belgian utility company to purchase two power plants in Ireland. AES dispatched an American employee, Chris Hollingshead, to transplant its values to Ireland. The joint venture is a financial success, but it has been a cultural struggle.

Irish managers who have worked their way up to the top of the company find the new management culture frustrating. They don't like standing by and watching front-line workers make decisions. When operators suggested replacing an expensive steel pipe with an inexpensive plastic one, they resisted. They feared the plastic pipe would last only a few days but the operators were convinced that plastic would do the job and they put the pipe in. That was a year ago and it's showing no signs of wear.

But the managers fear that if you give up control, you're no longer required. And to make matters worse, the plant didn't just have to change – it had to shrink as well. Hollingshead suggested announcing one big layoff and then moulding the people who remained into a tightly knit team. But he left the final decision up to the local management. They chose a voluntary-redundancy programme instead. Not enough workers volunteered, which forced them to come up with other offers. Every time another scheme was launched, there was a feeling of dread. The necessary workforce reduction is now complete, but it took five years.

The Belfast plant has adopted the AES culture – slowly. Too slowly for AES's CEO Dennis Bakke: 'The managers just didn't trust the workers enough to turn over power,' he says.

FILE 16

UNIT 4 Strategy 7, p41

This is Professor Clayton Christensen's solution to the dilemma presented by disruptive technologies.

to **go after** to chase, to follow in order to catch

to **survive** to continue to live
under threat at risk

Disruptive technologies

'There are lots of markets under threat from disruptive technologies. E-commerce in general disrupts retailing, so for example, we've seen on-line stockbrokers threatening the established financial service industry.

The solution is to set up a different company that has a different focus – and then let it go after the disruptive technology. Let the mainstream company keep doing what it's doing well – it's got to do that in order to survive, and you don't want it to lose that focus.

Acquiring companies with the disruptive technologies is also a solution, if you do it early enough. But, historically, the leading companies didn't sense how dangerous it was until it was too late. So part of the problem is just knowing that this is a threat.'

Tapescript

Unit 1
Exchanging
information

1.1

A   Tony, have you met Akiko Yano? Akiko, this is Tony Veluti.

B   Nice to meet you, Akiko.

C   And you. You work in the Rome office, don't you, Tony?

B   Yes, I've been working there for a couple of years now.

C   And what do you do exactly?

B   I work with our consultants, scheduling their assignments.

C   So it's not a hands-on technical job?

B   No, my background's engineering but most of my time's spent managing people these days.

A   I expect it's the same for you too, Akiko?

C   Not really. I work with ideas more than people – creative stuff.

B   What are you working on at the moment?

C   A logistics project. We're looking for ways to get things to customers quicker and cheaper.

B   Are you looking at the delivery process?

C   Yes, but we're also working on the design and ordering process. Everything really.

1.2

A   Why are Hamer guitars so good?

B   There're a lot of reasons. The wood's very important, and we pay a lot of attention to detail. We only make three guitars a day, you know.

A   Just three? How many people work here?

B   Ten. We used to employ more but we've concentrated on getting smaller over the years.

A   So, do you mean you wanted to get smaller?

B   You got it. It means we can focus on quality. Everyone here's a skilled craftsperson and we take a lot of pride in our work.

A   How much will that guitar cost?

B   This one?

A   Yes, when it's finished.

B   Around $2,000.

A   Ah.

B   All the carving's done by hand, but the other thing is the cost of the wood. When we buy the wood from the mill, we pay a 15% surcharge for the right to be able to pick and choose. We select the better looking, lighter weight wood. But even then, when it arrives, we only keep about 30%.

A   So you reject more than two thirds of each shipment?

B   That's right. And there are lots of extra costs involved there. First, we have to bear the costs of shipping the wood to our factory, and then the costs of shipping 70% of it back. It represents something like a 40–50% increase in the costs of our wood.

A   Mmm.

B   And then there's the time it takes. The wood selection has to be done by highly-trained people who know exactly what they're doing.

A   Uhuh.

B   But it's worth it. It's the wood that makes our guitars sound so good.

A   Yes.

B   They're the best production-made guitars you can find.

1.3

1   Good morning everyone. It's great to be in Boston today. Thank you for inviting me. As you know, I've been asked to share some ideas on the Dana Corporation management style. I'll be happy to take questions at the end, but before I get going, can I ask you all a question? How many of you have heard of the Dana Corporation? Can you raise your hand if you have? Excellent. Thank you. OK, for those that don't know us, I'd like to begin with a very brief overview of Dana. We'll look at who we are, what we do, and how we do it. OK. So, who is Dana? Dana is one of the largest automotive component suppliers in the world – last year we reported sales of $13.2 billion. We employ more than 82,000 people in thirty-two countries in some 320 facilities ...

2   ... you see, success in business is 10% money and 90% people. As I was just saying, our philosophy is: 'People are our most important asset.' And that brings me to my next point: we believe in education, participation, and innovation. We promote from within and our goal is at least forty hours of education per year for every person in Dana. We even have our own university and I'd like to show you some statistics about that. Now, you know what people say about statistics, don't you? 43.3% of statistics are meaningless. Well, here are some that are very meaningful. As you can see from this table, we've had 53,000 participants at Dana University to date, and 147 of our people have received MBAs ...

3   ... and that's why we always say: communicate, communicate, communicate. OK, let's turn to our ideas programme now and this is

very exciting. The Dana ideas programme is much more than a simple suggestion scheme. Every person in our organization is encouraged to submit at least two ideas for improvements per month and we implement 80% of them. Think about it. Two ideas a month, times 82,000 employees worldwide – that's more than two million ideas per year – two million ways to improve quality, productivity, and efficiency. Let's look at an example of how this works. In one Dana facility, we had an assembly worker who noticed that ...

1.4

A Thanks for listening. I'll take some questions now. Yes. Yukiko?
B What's the ship date for this release?
A It's July 2nd.
C Wasn't it June?
A Sorry, what was that, Alessandro?
C I thought the ship date was some time in June.
A Yes, it was June 4th originally, but we had to delay it until July 2nd. Jan?
D The last two releases were delayed as well. What's causing this problem?
A Are you asking about this release, or the previous releases?
D This one.
A That's tough to answer in a few words, but basically it's a development problem. You see, this product is coming out simultaneously in thirty-one countries, and nine languages, so it's very complicated. Yukiko again.
B Are these development problems getting worse? I mean, can we expect more delays in the future?
A I'm afraid so. As our products become more complex, they require more work. The effect of that is longer development schedules.
E But we lose customers to our competitors when we miss release dates.
A Yes. We realize it's a serious problem and we're solving it as fast as we can.

E Who is responsible for these delays?
A I think the important question is: what are we doing about it.
D Yes, could you tell us what steps you're taking to deal with this?
A I'm glad you asked me that. We're just about finished with a study of the development process and we're going to make changes. We're looking for short cuts and ways to make improvements ...

Unit 2
Sharing ideas

2.1

A OK everyone. We need ideas for a name.
C Well, I think we should call it *Hair* ...
A Hold on a moment, Peter. We'd better appoint someone to take notes before we begin.
B I can do that.
A Thanks, Yumi. OK. Let's start with the message. What message do we want to convey with this name? What should it say? Roberto?
D It needs to say 'This product is exciting.'
C It needs to say what the product does.
D It needs to convey sex appeal ...
C No, it needs to convey information.
A Hang on, Peter. Shall we let Roberto finish?
D Yes, I can speak from experience, you know. I'm a potential user.
A Yes, what would make you want to buy this product, Roberto?
D Excitement and sex appeal.
A So the name should say 'You're attractive now, but you'll be even more attractive if you use this product'?
D Exactly.
C Attractive now?
A Yes, men like Roberto are very attractive!
D How about trying to convey the idea of youth?
A Yes, good thinking.
D And success in your job? Using this product will be good for your career.

A Why don't we look for an 'executive' name?
D We could call it *Chief* ...
A Or *Top Man* ...
D Or *Boss Man* ...
A That's a good idea.
C I don't like it.
D Could we have a name that inspires confidence?
A Yes, why not something with a medical sound?
D Like *Zamtex* ...
A Or *Follitex*?
C No, that won't work.
A Is it a good idea to look for a masculine name?
D Like *Macho*?
A *Sportsman* ...
D *Tarzan* ...
C That's crazy!
A Crazy ideas are fine.
D Look, I don't think we should criticize one another's ideas at this stage.
B That's right. I'm noting them down so you can evaluate them later, Peter.
C But we're not saying what the product does. I think we should have a name that tells the consumer what's inside the bottle.
A *Hair Restorer*?
D *Hair Grow*?
A *Hair Return*?
D *Baldness Remedy*?
C Too old fashioned. Something up-to-date and immediate.
A What about *Hair Now*?
C No, I think we should call it: *Hair Today*.
D ... and gone tomorrow?
A We'd better not use that one.

2.2

I think we should give some of our shares to everyone in the company – and I mean everyone. Not just the managers, so the mail boy should get some and the tea lady should get some. That way, our stock will be wider spread. But there's something else. It's going to make everyone feel more committed. It means they'll care more and think about the value of what they're doing. Then we'll see huge benefits.

2.3

It's a nice idea, but I don't think it's viable. If we issued more shares, it would dilute the value of our stock. Feeling committed is a different issue. If people aren't working hard enough, we'll have to find another way to deal with the problem.

2.4

1   A   I said to him, 'I've told you before about this,' and he said, 'yes, I know you have,' and so I said ...
    B   Yes, thanks Stephen. Perhaps we could come back to this later if we have time.
    C   Speaking of time ...
    D   Do you have another appointment, then?
    C   Bank manager at 11.45.
    D   Overdrawn again?
    B   Can I remind everyone that I'm aiming to get through this by 11.30?
    A   Oh good, because I've got to call London.
    B   Yes, I know, Stephen. OK, let's turn to item three which is security. Heather, could you fill us in on the new procedures?
    C   Certainly, ...

2   B   We need to decide what we're going to do about the security camera suggestion.
    C   I think it's a great idea.
    A   Me too.
    C   Let's buy some more cameras then.
    A   How soon can we have them?
    B   Hold on, how do you feel about this, Martin?
    D   I don't think we should do this without getting several quotes first.
    B   Stephen?
    A   Yes, that's true. We should check out some other suppliers.
    C   How long will it take?
    B   Could you get some quotes by next Tuesday, Martin?
    D   Yep, no problem.
    B   Good. So Martin will get ... say three quotes for security cameras by next week and we'll review the matter at our next meeting ...

3   D   Are we wrapped up?
    B   Just a moment, is there anything else anyone wants to say?
    A   Is the meeting going to be at 11.00 again next week?
    B   Yes, is that a problem?
    A   I sometimes have to go to the other site on Tuesday mornings and it's a bit difficult to get here in time.
    D   Sounds like you need a faster car.
    C   I'm afraid I have another meeting at 2.00.
    A   Oh not to worry then.
    D   Just get up earlier on Tuesdays.
    A   Yeah.
    B   So are you saying it's not a problem, Stephen?
    A   Yes, I'll work something out.
    B   OK, so we've agreed that we'll meet at 11.00 again next Tuesday.
    A   Yes, fine.
    C   Are we finished then?
    D   Looks like it.
    B   Yes, this meeting is officially over.

Unit 3
Tackling problems

See page 24.

D   Debbie Hobbs.
G   Debbie? Hi, it's Gary in Jeddah.
D   Hey Gary. How's it going?
G   Fine thanks, but we've got a problem with our brake pads.
D   What's that?
G   I visited the plant where they're being installed today and they're complaining about them.
D   Don't they work?
G   No, they work fine. It's the way they're packed. It's difficult for the guys on the line to get them off the pallets and do their job.
D   How long has this been going on?
G   For a couple of weeks. They were all right before that apparently. Could you find out what our packaging people have been up to and let me know?

D   Of course. I'll look into it right away.
G   Good, and please get back to me as soon as you can.
D   What time is it there now?
G   It's 11 o'clock at night. I'm nine hours ahead of you here.
D   Then I'll try to get a quick answer. Which hotel are you in?
G   The Holiday Inn. The number's: 966 2 631 4000. I'm in room 664.
D   OK, leave it with me. I'll take care of it.
G   Great, thanks Debbie.

3.3

D   Hi Gary, it's Debbie.
G   Debbie? I was asleep. What time is it?
D   It's five o'clock here so it must be 2 a.m. your time. Sorry it's taken so long.
G   Never mind. What did you find out?
D   Apparently Logistics changed the stacking method last month. They found a way to get more brake pads onto the pallets.
G   I knew it! They should've checked with the customer first. Have you told them to change back?
D   Yes, but they're not happy about it.
G   Why not?
D   They want to save money on shipping costs.
G   Forget the shipping costs! The customer's talking about switching to another supplier.
D   It's OK. They've agreed to change back to the old system for the time being and I've set up a meeting for when you get back.
G   Good. Thanks Debbie. I'll go back to sleep, then.
D   You're welcome. Sweet dreams, Gary.

3.4

Hi, this is Peter Clark at Gencia Technologies. I'm afraid I'm unavailable at the moment, but if you need me urgently, press the star key now to send your telephone number to my pager screen. Or you can try to reach me on my cell phone at 202 555 7639. Otherwise, leave a message here and I'll get back to you as soon as I can.

3.5

Mr Clark, this is Carmen Santez. I'm very sorry about this but I'm afraid I've got to go back to Argentina earlier than planned, so I can't make our meeting on Friday. Could you give me a call? I'm in the Marriott Marquis Hotel – that's 212 398 1900 and my room number is 1147. Thank you very much.

3.6

PC Hello Ms Santez, this is Peter Clark of Gencia returning your call.
CS Ah, thank you for getting back to me so quickly. I'm sorry about Friday.
PC Oh that's all right. Would you like to reschedule?
CS I'd love to but my schedule's very tight as I'm leaving New York on Wednesday evening. Do you mind if I don't come down to Washington?
PC Would you like me to come up to New York instead?
CS Could you? That would make things a lot easier for me.
PC No problem. When would be good for you?
CS How are you fixed for Tuesday afternoon – say 2 o'clock?
PC That's fine for me.
CS Excellent. And would you mind coming to my hotel? I could book a meeting room.
PC That's great. I'll look forward to seeing you at the Marriott at 2 o'clock on Tuesday then.

3.7

See page 32.

3.8

C Global Rentals. Good morning.
B At last, a human being!
C I'm sorry?
B I've just spent half an hour trying to get through your automated answering system.
C Oh, I'm really sorry about that. How can I help you?
B I rented a car from your company in Las Vegas last month. I've just got my credit card bill and it seems you've charged me $390. I only had the car one day, so I don't understand why the bill's so high.
C $390 seems like a lot. May I have your name?
B Eliane Poitier.
C And you rented the car in Las Vegas. What date was that?
B March 7th and you billed American Express on the 14th.
C Yes, I'm just calling it up on my screen. OK. According to our records, you had the car for four days.
B That's strange. I only had it for four hours.
C What price did they give you when you checked the car back in?
B It was a Sunday so your office shut early. I returned the car to its spot and dropped the keys in the box.
C So you didn't talk to any of our people?
B No.
C Mmm. That's a problem.
B Look, I left Las Vegas on the Monday, so I couldn't have kept the car for four days.
C I don't suppose you've kept your air tickets?
B Yes, I have. Would you like me to send them to you?
A That'd be great. You see, I just need some documentation in case our management asks about this.

3.9

A There seems to be a mistake on this invoice.
B Oh, what's that?
A I'm afraid you've charged us for eight pieces but we only received six.
B That's strange. The delivery receipt says eight and it was signed.
A I don't suppose I could see a copy of that?
B Of course. Would you like me to fax it to you?

3.10

C We're sending these goods back so we'd like a refund.
D We'll be happy to do that but I'm afraid there'll be a twenty per cent handling fee.
C Oh? I didn't realize.
D Yes, it's in the contract – clause five I think.
C Twenty per cent seems like a lot.
D I'm afraid that's our standard charge for returns. We need to cover our costs, you see.

UNIT 4
Planning ahead

4.1

A Is it true that you're about to build a wind farm on Rider's Hill?
B We have no immediate plans, but we've been looking at a range of options and Rider's Hill is one of the best.
A So you do want to build on Rider's Hill?
B We're still testing the wind on Rider's Hill but we expect that the results will be favourable, yes. Next question?
C How many turbines would you like to build?
B The maximum number is twenty-two.
C And are you planning to build them next to Logan Road?
B Absolutely not. They'll be back from the road.
C So you're saying the turbines won't be visible?
B No, it's true that they'll be visible from the highest point of Logan Road. But they'll be insignificant in the wider landscape. Next?
D I have a different question. Are you intending to build a highway, too?
B No, we have no plans for that.
D Ah, then how are you going to get to the site?
B There's an existing farm road. It'll require minor upgrading for the construction vehicles, but that's all. If I could just say, ... this proposal has significant environmental benefits. We're aiming to reduce our fossil fuel consumption by twenty per cent over the next four years. Building this wind farm means we can reduce pollution elsewhere. Yes?
E How much power are you planning to produce?

B We estimate twenty-two turbines will produce around forty-two million kW hours a year. Now, an average house uses roughly 8,000 kW hours a year. So if we go ahead, we can look forward to enough electricity for about 5,000 homes.

F I live at the top of Logan Road and I'm worried about noise. Won't it be very noisy?

B The noise depends on the type of turbine and we're due to make a decision on that next week. But if you live at the top of Logan Road, I doubt if you'll be able to hear anything at all.

F What about safety?

B These turbines are designed and built to the highest safety standards. A passer-by runs more risk of being struck by lightning than they do …

4.2

Good evening, and welcome to the business news tonight.

Connect-X CEO, Harrison Kincaid, announced this morning that the company has signed contracts worth seven billion dollars in the last two weeks. Connect-X will be supplying advanced light-based high-speed components to four major computer companies.

The Transportation Safety Agency reports six drivers were seriously injured this week by exploding hydrogen gas in the new H2 electric car. The vehicles were being used in market tests and H2 says it is stopping tests until further research is completed.

Scientists are reporting doubts about Empraxo's new cancer drug, Zumoxin. Results from clinical trials suggest that negative side effects include weakness, blood loss, and weight loss.

Virtware reports third quarter sales have rocketed following the introduction of its downloadable virtual pet products. With just three weeks to go till Christmas, the company's website has become almost inaccessible because of the large numbers of on-line buyers.

And that's all from the business news team tonight.

4.3

Stocks increased all around the world today. Tokyo, Frankfurt, and Zurich were all up 4% and the London and New York exchanges closed up 5%.

The top-traded company today was the computer component manufacturer Connect-X. Connect-X closed at $300 a share after announcing $7 billion worth of new sales contracts. Another surprise winner was Virtware, the web-based virtual pet company, which solved its on-line access problems and had a huge Christmas success. Virtware's share prices doubled to close at $200.

But it was a bad day for the drug giant, Empraxo. Empraxo's share prices were cut in half following negative test reports on its cancer drug, Zumoxin. Empraxo closed at $50. But the big loser today was H2, whose share prices fell to just one dollar. H2 filed for bankruptcy this afternoon to protect itself from injury lawsuits resulting from its market tests.

4.4

A It's a tight deadline and we're under a lot of pressure.

B Are you still on budget?

A Yes, and everything's on track. In fact we're slightly ahead of schedule.

B Good.

A But I don't know for how long. There's a management review meeting tomorrow and when they see the design, I think they'll want to change it.

B They wanted a simple design so it runs faster, right?

A They did. But it doesn't look very exciting.

B They haven't seen it yet?

A No. They won't see it until we run the demo tomorrow. I'm sure they'll want to change the look and feel.

B What will that mean?

A We'll probably have to double the graphics budget.

B Ouch!

A And it'll put another 15,000 onto design work costs too. But the other thing is the schedule. It'll set us back.

B Is there anything you can do about it?

A Well, I have one idea. If we can remove some of the content, I can shift some of that money into graphics.

B They might agree to that.

A I need to move 50,000 from content to graphics development …

B Get the figures ready, in case they want to see them tomorrow.

A Yes, I will.

B What about the technical implementation budget?

A That stays the same, unless …

B Unless what?

A Unless the site gets more hits than we planned for. That'll blow the budget. We'll have to buy more servers.

Unit 5
Resolving conflict

5.1

1 Those chocolates look nice.
2 You said you'd be here by eight.
3 Are you busy?
4 Is anybody else here feeling hot?
5 Goodness, is that the time?
6 Is that your car in my parking space?
7 I thought I put a cup of coffee down here.
8 You should have been with us last night!
9 I liked most parts of your proposal.

5.2

A I thought we could start around ten.

B It's no problem for me to come earlier.

A No, ten o'clock is fine, then I'll introduce you to the team.

B OK, em, will there be a chance to take a tour of the warehouse?

A We'll pass through it on our way to the restaurant.

B Restaurant?

A Yes, we've got an excellent French restaurant just a block away. I thought we could go there for lunch.

B I've heard you had a really nice company cafeteria.

A Yes, we have, but before we go to the restaurant, we can meet Laura Berne.

B Have you been able to arrange a meeting with Julio Ramon, too?

A Yes.

B Because it would be good if I could meet him before Laura Berne.

A He's available in the afternoon, so we'll have lunch, review the sales figures, and then you can meet him.

B The sales figures?

A Yes. Is that a problem?

B I didn't realize we had to review the sales figures too.

A I thought you'd like to. And then we'll have a final meeting with Mr Fliedner, the department head.

B What time will that be?

A Four o'clock.

B I see. The traffic starts getting heavy around that time, doesn't it?

A I'm afraid so. So anyway, does that sound all right?

5.3

B You should see this schedule!

C Why, what's the problem?

B I wanted to make an early start so I could leave early and avoid the traffic, but he's got me starting at ten. And he's scheduled the meeting with Julio after the meeting with Laura, which is the wrong way around.

C Why didn't you tell him?

B He didn't listen. I said I wanted to check out the warehouse, but he arranged a review of the sales figures instead.

C Too bad.

5.4

I've been doing my job for ten years and I love it. It's interesting and challenging and I'm good at it. But now my company has asked me to lead a new venture it's starting. It's a 'virtual' university. It's going to provide distance learning courses via computers for our company's employees. I've never done anything like this before and I'd have to give up my current job to do it.

5.5

Last year, I left my job and started my own software company. I've developed a new product that's technically superior to anything else on the market. But it isn't ready to ship yet and meanwhile, the competition is increasing. Several new products like mine have been launched and I don't even have a marketing team yet. Should I be trying to get it to market as soon as possible? Or should I be trying to sell my company and the new technology to a larger software company instead?

5.6

A How many do you think they can sell?

B I intend to ask them that question.

A Yes, but what do you think their answer will be?

B Maybe 2,000 in the first year?

A That's good. And we can offer to increase the discount if they sell more.

B Yes, we need to work out a sliding scale. But I think the main problem is going to be the length of the contract. If they want two or three years ...

A We should avoid making any long-term agreements like that.

B Yes, you see, I can't help thinking we might be better off saying 'no' to these people.

A What are our options if we can't reach an agreement?

B We can keep looking. There are other distributors, but we can't afford to take too long.

5.7

B Would you like to start things off?

C Sure. What would you like to know?

B Tell us everything. We're here to listen.

C Well, why don't I begin with what

we need? First, we need to have control over the pricing of the bicycles in American stores.

B That's going to be a problem, but please go on.

C We'd like to have a three-year contract – exclusive.

B This could be a very short meeting, but tell me more. How many do you think you can sell?

C 10,000.

B So you're saying 10,000 – over three years?

C No, 10,000 a year.

B Ah, well that changes things a little. Going back to the pricing.

C Yes?

B You mentioned having control, and I wonder how important that is. You see, we'd prefer to set the prices because we've managed to carve a high-end niche in our home market and we need to maintain an up-market position ...

Language notes

❯ Tenses and verb forms

Present

The most common tense in spoken and written English is the present. The *simple present* is the most common form and we can use it to talk about permanent situations and things we do on a regular basis.

*I **live** in the Netherlands.*
*Hamer only **makes** three guitars a day.*
*Where **do** you **work**?*
***Does** your company **have** an employee suggestion scheme?*

We can use the *present continuous* to talk about temporary actions that are in progress now or happening around the time of speaking.

*I'm **calling** the file up on my screen.*
*What's **causing** this problem?*
*How **are** you **doing** with that report?*

We use the *present perfect* to talk about past actions that have present importance.

*It's the best presentation I've ever **seen**.* (Up until now.)
*We've **achieved** huge reductions in costs.* (Our costs are now lower.)
*What **have** you **done** to the packaging?* (It's causing problems now.)
*I've **been working** for IBM for 8 years.* (I still work here.)
*How long **has** she **been waiting**?* (She's still waiting.)

Notice that the *present perfect simple* can be used to talk about actions that were completed in the past while the *present perfect continuous*

is used for actions that began in the past and are still continuing now as in the last two examples.

Past

The most common form of the past tense is the *simple past* and we use it to talk about many different types of past events.

*Peter Guber **founded** his own movie company in 1995.* (a finished past action)
*I **worked** for Cisco for two years.* (a regular activity that is over now)
*We **called** an emergency meeting and we **asked** everyone to come.* (events in a story)

We use the *past continuous* when we talk about an activity that was in progress at a particular time in the past.

*You didn't answer your phone. What **were** you **doing**?* (at the time of my call)
*We **were having** problems with the budget so we called a meeting.* (There were ongoing problems so a meeting was called.)

We use the *past perfect* to show that one event happened before another in the past.

*I'd **taken** the phone off the hook when you tried to call.* (First I took the phone off the hook, then you tried to call.)
*We **had run** into problems with our budget, so we called a meeting.* (The budget problems existed before we called the meeting.)

Continuous forms

We use *continuous* verb forms when we see an event as temporary or ongoing.

I'm staying at the Marriot. (It's a temporary activity.)
As I was saying … (It's an ongoing activity and not completed.)
We've been working on an environmental project. (It's a temporary activity and it may still be ongoing, rather than completed.)

Compare these sentences:
I work for General Electric. (It's my regular job. I work there permanently.)
I'm working for General Electric. (It's a temporary job that is in progress now.)

We went bankrupt when she became CEO. (She probably caused the bankruptcy – it happened after she became CEO.)
We were going bankrupt when she became CEO. (She probably didn't cause the bankruptcy – we started going bankrupt before she became CEO.)

I've written the contract. (The contract is completed.)
I've been writing the contract. (The contract is probably not completed.)

Perfect forms

We use *perfect verb forms* when we see the time of an event as being earlier than some other time or event in the present, past, or future.

Has she spoken to you about the meeting? (Did she speak to you before now?)
It was too late to make changes. We'd already signed the contract. (The contract was signed before we wanted to change it.)
I'll have finished the report by Friday. (before Friday)

Compare these sentences:
Do you hold brainstorming meetings? (on a regular basis)

Have you held brainstorming meetings? (before now)

Management made changes. The project went over budget. (The changes probably caused problems.)
Management made changes. The project had gone over budget. (The problems existed before the changes.)

We're making progress. (It's happening now.)
We've been making progress. (We started making progress before now.)

You should contact the customer. (now or in the future)
You should have contacted the customer. (before now)

The future

We use many different language forms to talk about the future.

Will is the most common and we often use it to make predictions.

In the future computers will translate all our documents.

The contracted form of will is *'ll* and the negative form is *won't*.

It'll be much more cost effective. We won't have to pay translators.

Going to is also common and we can use it to talk about intentions.

Are you going to employ an interpreter?

We also use present tenses to talk about the future. We use the *present continuous* to talk about planned arrangements.

I'm interviewing a candidate at ten o'clock.

We use the *simple present* to talk about timetabled events and schedules.

*My flight **leaves** at six o'clock.*

There are a lot of other ways of talking about the future. There are verbs we can use to express feelings:
*We **want/hope/would like** to visit your plant.*
*We **look forward** to seeing you on the 14th.*

There are verbs that express intentions:
*We **intend/plan/aim** to launch the new version next month.*

There are verbs that express how certain we feel:
*I **doubt** if it'll work.*
*We don't **expect** any more delays.*
*We **estimate** the cost will be $3,000.*

There are also expressions we can use to indicate when something will happen:
*They're **due to** move into the new offices on 14th July.* (The date is planned.)
*We're **about to** open a new office in Turin.* (It will happen very soon.)

Modals

Must, may, might, can, could, will, would, shall, should, and *ought to* are modal verbs. They add extra meaning to other verbs to show the speaker's attitude or opinion. Usually the meanings are connected with ability and possibility, obligation, necessity, or certainty.

***Can** you hear me at the back?* (Are you able to hear me?)
***Could** you give me a hand?* (Is it possible?)
***Should** we focus our energies on this?* (Is it necessary?)
*Management **might** make changes.* (I think it's a possibility.)
*We **will** find a solution.* (I'm certain.)

Modal verbs can have more than one meaning.

*It's two o'clock so it **must** be midnight in Jeddah.* (I'm pretty certain.)
*I **must** go. I'm late.* (It's necessary for me to go.)

In addition to *must, should,* and *ought to,* we also use: *have to, have got to,* and *need to* to express obligation. *Have to* is more common than *must,* particularly in spoken English.

Must, have to, have got to, and *need to* express strong obligation. *Should* and *ought to* express weaker obligation.

*We **have to** do it.* (I think it's essential.)
*We **should** do it.* (I think it's the right thing to do.)

Notice the negative forms of these verbs have different meanings. We use *mustn't, shouldn't,* and *ought not to* to say it's wrong to do something. But we use *don't have to, haven't got to,* and *don't need to* to say something isn't necessary.

*Hurry up. We **mustn't** be late.* (It's important not to be late.)
*We have plenty of time. You **don't have to** hurry.* (It's not necessary to hurry.)

❯ Conditionals

We commonly use *if* to state conditions.

***If** you buy 300 pieces, we'll increase your discount.*

There are other words we can use to state conditions, such as *unless, when, in case,* and *until.*

*We can't increase the discount **unless** you buy 300.* (*Unless* has a similar meaning to *if not.*)
***When** you buy 300, we'll increase the discount.* (You're certain to buy 300 at some future time.)
*We won't increase the discount **until** you order 300.* (You have to wait.)

We'll make a few extra, in case you need them later. (It's a precaution because you might need them later.)

Notice how *in case* is used to talk about precautions.

Conditional sentences formed with the simple present and *will* are commonly called the *first conditional*.

*If I **like** the salary, I'**ll take** the job.*

But we use a wide variety of other verb forms to make conditional sentences.

*If it'**s** not fun, **don't do** it.*
*You **can't be** creative if you **don't take** risks.*
***Could** you **raise** your hand if you'**ve heard** this before.*
*If his plane **was delayed**, he'**ll have missed** his connection.*

We can use *second* and *third conditional* forms to talk about more imaginary or hypothetical situations. These conditionals contain past tense verb forms and indicate a distance from present reality.

We can use the *second conditional* to talk about imaginary or hypothetical situations in the future. They might be future situations that are possible, but very unlikely to happen.

*If Amazon.com **offered** me a job, I'**d ask** for stock options.*

Or they might be situations that couldn't possibly happen in the future.

*If I **had** the power, I'**d hire** a consultant to do this job.*

We can use the *third conditional* to talk about imaginary situations in the past and hypothesize about things that didn't happen.

*If she **hadn't accepted** the job, she **would have regretted** it.* (But she did accept the job.)

❯ Indirect forms

Levels of formality in English depend on who we're communicating with and what we are doing, but there are no strict rules. To avoid being impolite, we use a variety of indirect forms.

Indirect questions are often used at the start of conversations, or to ask for more sensitive information. We *don't* use the verb *do* to form indirect questions.

Direct: *How much **does** it cost?*
Indirect: *Could you tell me how much it costs?*

The word order changes in indirect questions.

Direct: *What time **is it**?*
Indirect: *Do you know what time **it is**?*

When the answer to a question is *yes* or *no*, we use *if*, or *whether*.

*Do you know **whether** the flight's on time?*
*Could you tell me **if** the flight's delayed?*

We often use 'distancing' forms to avoid imposing on people:

Could you get me a coffee? (Get me a coffee.)
Would you mind calling back tomorrow? (Call me tomorrow.)

We might drop hints instead of making direct requests:
That coffee smells good! (Can I have a cup?)
Is anybody else here cold? (Could I shut the window?)

When complaining, we might avoid direct criticism and suggest that we are a little uncertain.

*There **seems** to be a problem with this invoice.* (You've made a mistake.)
*That **seems** a bit expensive.* (Your price is unreasonable.)

❯ Passives

Passives are common when we're thinking about what's done or happens to something or someone, rather than what the thing or person does. It's formed by using the appropriate tense of the verb *be* and the past participle form of the main verb.

*Penicillin **has saved** millions of lives.* (Active – the focus is on what penicillin has done.)
*Penicillin **was discovered** by Fleming.* (Passive – the focus is on what happened to penicillin.)
*Her flight **arrived** late.* (Active – the focus is on what the flight did.)
***Has** her flight **been delayed**?* (Passive – the focus is on what has happened to the flight.)

❯ Vocabulary

Collocations

A collocation is two or more words which have a strong tendency to be used together. For example, the verb *turn off* is commonly used with the noun *light*, so *turn off the light* is a collocation.

We can say:
***turn off** the light* BUT NOT *close the light*

Close might be possible in other languages, but it doesn't occur in English.

Similarly, the adjectives *strong* and *heavy* both commonly occur with the noun *competition*, so these expressions are both collocations:
strong competition AND *heavy competition*

But notice we can't use the adjectives *hard* or *large* in the same way:
NOT *hard competition* OR *large competition*

There is no special grammatical reason why we don't use these words together. It's a matter of custom and they sound wrong together.

This means that when you're learning a new English word, you need to pay attention to the other words around it. For example, if you are learning the verb *to delegate*, it's useful to note that we often use it with the word *responsibility*. If you're learning the noun *initiative* it's helpful to note it's commonly used with the verb *take*:

to delegate responsibility
to take initiative

Noting down phrases like this, instead of single words, can make it easier to remember new words and learn how to use them correctly.

Countable and uncountable nouns

We see *countable nouns* as separate items. They have plural forms and we can use them with words and expressions like *a/an*, *many*, *a few*, and *a couple of*.

*a suggestion, **a few** thoughts, **a couple of** ideas*
*We haven't received **many** suggestions.*

We see *uncountable nouns* as a mass that cannot be separated. They have no plural form and we use them with words and expressions like *much*, *a little*, and *a piece of*.

***a little** help, **a piece of** advice*
*We haven't done **much** research.*

Languages differ and some nouns that are countable in your language may be uncountable in English. Here are some nouns that often cause confusion. They are all uncountable in English: *money, equipment, information, traffic, pollution, work, employment, advice, research, news, data*. Notice how they are used with singular verb forms.

*Is the **equipment** working?*
*There **wasn't** enough **money**.*

Adjectives and adverbs

We use adjectives to describe the qualities people or things have.

*a **wild** idea; a **creative** company*

Adjectives ending in *-ed* generally describe how people feel.

*He was interest**ed**/bor**ed**/excit**ed**, etc.*

Adjectives ending in *-ing* generally describe the people or things that caused the feelings.

*His job was very interest**ing**/bor**ing**/excit**ing**, etc.*

Adverbs add more information about a verb or adjective regarding manner, time, place, degree, etc.

*We can deliver **quickly/cheaply/immediately/soon/tomorrow**, etc.*
*I'm **terribly/really/quite** tired.*

Many adverbs are formed by adding *-ly* to adjectives.

*She's a **quick** worker. She works **quickly**.*

But there are some important exceptions:

*She's a **fast/hard/good/worker**. She works **fast/hard/well**.*

Gerunds and infinitives

Gerunds follow prepositions in a lot of common expressions.

*How about **meeting** at eight?*
*We're interested in **hearing** more.*
*I look forward to **seeing** you on Friday.*

Certain verbs, like *avoid*, can be followed by a gerund but not an infinitive.

*We should avoid **making** any long term agreements.*
BUT NOT ~~We should avoid **to make** any long term agreements.~~

Other verbs like this include:
finish, enjoy, dislike, give up, deny, suggest, delay, put off, carry on, go on, keep (on), can't help, risk, postpone, consider

Certain verbs, like *offer*, can be followed by an infinitive but not a gerund.

*We can offer **to increase** their discount.*
BUT NOT ~~We can offer **increasing** their discount.~~

Other verbs like this are:
decide, want, plan, manage, choose, promise, agree, can't afford, refuse, fail, learn

Say and tell

Saying is about speaking words.

Could you say that again?

So we often use *say* with the actual words spoken.

*He **said**, 'Goodbye.'*

Telling is about giving information or orders.

*She **told** us how to get to the office.*
*He **told** us to hurry up.*

In many situations we can use either *say* or *tell*. But notice *tell* is followed by the person being told. *Say* isn't.

*She told **me** the flight was delayed.*
She said the flight was delayed.

There are some other common expressions where we use *tell* as well.

Is he telling the truth/lies?
I can't tell the difference between an American and a Canadian accent.

Glossary

to be **about to** do something to be on the point of doing something very soon

to **accelerate** to go faster; to make something go faster

adequate enough for what's needed

administration the day-to-day management and organization of business activities

an **agenda** a list of things to discuss at a meeting

ahead of schedule to have done more than was planned

to **annoy** to make somebody fairly angry; to irritate

apparently according to what people say

to **appoint** someone to choose somebody for a job

an **asset** a useful or valuable thing that a company has or owns

to **avoid** doing something to prevent something from happening

a **back-up plan** a second plan that you have in case the first plan doesn't work

bankrupt the state of not having enough money to pay your debts

to **base** something on to do or develop something using particular information as a starting point or source

to **bear costs** to accept responsibility for payment

to **beat** to do better than someone or something; to win. Also you can't beat – you can't do or get better than …

a **bid** an offer to pay a sum of money in order to buy something. Also to bid

to **blame** to think or say that someone is responsible for something bad that has happened

a **booth** a small enclosed space with thin walls that divide it from the rest of the space or area

a **boundary** a limit; something that stops you from going further

to **brainstorm** to solve problems by asking all the members of a group to think of as many ideas as possible

brief short

a **budget** a sum of money that is set aside for a particular purpose, e.g. the training budget or a target to be reached, e.g. We didn't achieve the sales budget. Also to go over budget – to spend more money than planned or agreed; to blow a budget – to overspend by a large amount

capital an amount of money you invest in a new business

to **carve** to cut wood in the pattern of a design. Also to carve a market niche – to create a place that is yours in a section of a market, often through hard work

in **case** because something might happen, e.g. Take an umbrella in case it rains.

CEO (abbreviation) Chief Executive Officer

CFO (abbreviation) Chief Financial Officer

to **chair** to be the chairperson at a meeting

to **chase** to run after something

to **close at** to finish the day's trading on the stock market at a certain price

a **code** a group of numbers used for identification, e.g. 44 is the dialling code for the UK. Also see dress code

collaboration working together, especially to create or produce something

committed giving a lot of your time and attention to something because you think it is right or important

a **component** one of several parts which together make the whole of something

a **compromise** an agreement that is reached when each side allows the other side part of what it wanted. Also to compromise

to **concentrate on** to focus your attention on something

a **concession** something you agree to do or give up in order to end an argument. Also to concede – to give something up

to **consent** to agree to something

to **convey** to communicate something; to make ideas, thoughts, or feelings known. Also to carry something from one place to another

to **cool off** to calm down

corruption dishonest, illegal behaviour, especially by someone in authority

to **count on someone** to rely or depend on someone

a **craftsperson** a person who makes things skilfully, especially with their hands

a **cubicle** a small box-like compartment that people work in

a **deadline** a time or date before which something must be done

to **delegate** to give somebody with a lower job or rank tasks to perform

a **demo** showing how something works, short for demonstration

a **deposit** an amount of money paid when you rent or hire something, which is later returned to you if the item is not damaged

a **device** something, often a tool or machine, that is made for a particular use or purpose

a **dilemma** a situation in which you have to make a difficult choice between two or more things

diligent showing care and effort in your work

to **dilute** to make weaker

a **discount** a price reduction. Also *to discount* – to reduce prices

to **dispatch** to send

disposable intended to be thrown away after being used once or for a short time

to **disrupt** to disturb; to stop a situation, event, etc., from continuing in its normal way. Also *disruptive* – causing disturbance

to **doubt** to think that something is unlikely or to feel uncertain about something

to **download** to copy computer files from the Internet onto a local machine

down-market cheaper and lower quality. Also *to move down-market* – to shift focus to cheaper and lower-quality products

a **dress code** standards or guidelines for the clothes that people can wear

to **dumb down** to make stupid; to reduce the level of knowledge required to understand something

due expected or planned to happen

dynamic active; full of energy and ideas

to **earn** to get money by working or as a return on an investment

e-commerce buying and selling over the Internet

effective producing the result that you want

efficient working well and quickly; producing a good result in the minimum time

to **enable** to make possible

to **encourage** to give support, hope, or confidence to somebody

to be **entitled to** having the right to have or do something

an **entrepreneur** someone who starts a company

equity the value of the shares issued by a company

an **estimate** a calculation of the likely cost of something

exclusive not to be shared; just for you

to **execute** to do or perform what has been planned

expanding getting larger

to **explode** to burst with a loud noise. Also *explosive* – a substance that can explode, e.g. dynamite

face saving protecting someone's feelings and pride

to **facilitate** to make something possible or easier. Also a *facility* – a building used for a particular purpose

fault responsibility for a mistake, e.g. *Whose fault is it?*

favourable good; supportive to the plan. In American English: *favorable*

a **fee** a charge made for providing a service

to **fill** someone **in** to give someone information about something

a **founder** someone who founds or starts a company

frank showing your thoughts and feelings openly; saying what you mean

to **freeze** to stop something changing for a period of time, e.g. prices

a **front-line worker** a worker engaged in performing tasks rather than managing them

fulfilling satisfying your hopes and dreams

funds available money

furious very angry

to **gamble** to do something which involves risk

to **gather** to collect

generous larger than usual. Also willing to give more help, money, etc., than is usual or necessary

to **get acquainted** with someone to get to know someone

to **get along** to proceed; to perform

to **get even** with someone to get revenge

to **get going** to begin

to **get through** something to complete; to finish

a **giant** something that is very large

globalization the process of extending business operations and activities worldwide

to **go after** to chase; to follow in order to catch

to **go out of your way** to put in extra effort in order to help someone

a **hacker** a person who breaks into other people's computer systems without permission

hasty quick and without enough thought

to **head up** to lead

a **hint** an idea that is suggested in an indirect way

a **hit** a visit to a website

to **hit on** to discover

huge very large

to **ignore** to pay no attention to something or somebody

an **image** an impression that is given to the public

an **impact** an effect

to **implement** to start using an idea, a system, etc. Also *implementation* – putting a plan or system into operation

inaccessible not possible to be reached or entered

in case see *case*

Inc (abbreviation) Incorporated

an **income** the money you receive regularly as payment for your work or from other sources

inconvenient causing difficulty or problems

inevitable cannot be avoided or prevented from happening

ingenious cleverly thought out or made

initiative a personal decision to solve a problem or make improvements

injured hurt; harmed. Also *an injury lawsuit* – a legal argument in a court of law where one person wants money from another because the other person injured them

innovation the introduction of new things or ideas

insignificant small and not important

to **inspire** to give somebody a feeling of being able to do something good

integrity being truthful and having firm moral ideas

an **interface** the way a computer program accepts information from or provides it to a user

an **interpreter** a person whose job it is to translate what someone is saying immediately into another language

inventory the goods a company has in stock at a particular time

IT (abbreviation) information technology

an **item** a single thing on a list, e.g. *item four on the agenda*

jargon special and technical words that are used by a particular group of people that other people do not understand

labour workers; the workforce. Also the work done by a group of workers. In American English: *labor*

to **lack** to have too little or none of something

a **lap top** (computer) a small computer that's easy to carry around and that can use batteries for power

large-scale involving many things and people

a **launch** the introduction of a new product to a market. Also *to launch* – to start something new

a **layoff** telling workers you will no longer employ them. Also to *lay* workers *off*

lead time the time between placing an order and receiving a product

to **let** to allow

likely probable

logistics the organization of supplies and services for a complex operation

to **lose sight of** to forget

low-end bottom of a range

a **margin** the amount of profit that a company makes on something

to **mass produce** to produce in large quantities

maternity connected with women who are going to have or have just had a baby

a **mill** a building containing machinery to process products like wood, paper, or steel

to **minimize** to make something as small as possible. Also *miniaturization* – the act of making things on a much smaller scale

a **mission** a particular task or duty that you feel you should do

to **monitor** to check, record, and watch something

a **moral** a lesson on the right way to behave that can be learnt from a story

to **mortgage** to use property, e.g. a house, as security for a loan

to **mould** to shape

multinational existing in or involving many countries

mundane ordinary, not interesting or exciting

a **nap** a short sleep

negligence not being careful enough; lack of care

to **negotiate** to bargain; to reach an agreement by discussion

to **network** to develop contacts with people working in the same field

to **obstruct** to stop something from happening or moving

to **offend** to upset; to hurt

an **option** an alternative

an **outcome** the result or situation at the end of an activity or event

outrageous shocking, making you very angry

to **outsource** to pay another company to supply services

to be **overdrawn** having spent more money than you have in your bank account

overheads indirect costs; the regular costs of running a business, such as salaries, rent, telephone bills, etc.

to **overspend** to spend more than planned

an **overview** a short general description without much detail

a **pallet** a flat wooden platform for carrying goods

a **paradox** a statement that seems to be impossible but that is or may be true

a **parent** a company that controls other smaller companies or subsidiaries

participation taking part in something

a **PC** (abbreviation) personal computer

a **perk** a benefit

a **perspective** the way you think about something; your point of view

to **pick and choose** to select very carefully, rejecting a lot

a **plant** a factory

a **portfolio** a collection of investments owned by a person or group

to **postpone** to delay

potential may possibly become something, e.g. a *potential customer*

preferential giving or showing better treatment to one person or group than to others

pretty very, but not completely

to **price** to set the price of something

to take **pride** in something to feel pleased and proud because you do something well

primary most important; main

a **profit** the money made by a business; total sales minus total costs (if this figure is positive). Also *profitable/unprofitable* – making/failing to make a profit

promising showing signs of being very good or successful

to **promote** to move someone to a higher position or more important job

to **protect** to defend something; to keep something safe

publicly-traded a company having shares bought and sold on the stock market

to **pursue** to find out more about something; to continue with something

to **put down** to say something to make someone seem foolish or stupid

to **put up with** to tolerate

to **quit** to leave a job (informal)

a **quote** a price estimate, short for *quotation*. Also *to quote* – e.g. a price

radical very great or important, e.g. *radical changes*

a **range** a variety or selection of things that belong to the same group

rapidly very quickly

to **reassess** to calculate again; to rethink

a **receipt** a piece of paper that is given to show that you have paid for or received something

recognition appreciation and acknowledgement for an achievement or ability

a **recruit** someone selected to join an organization. Also *to recruit*

redundancy losing your job because there is no work for you. Also *to make redundant*

a **referral** passing on a contact for someone else to deal with

to **regard** to think of somebody or something (in the way mentioned)

reimbursement repayment of a cost. Also *to reimburse*

a **release** something made available to the public, e.g. *press release*, *software release*. Also *to release*

relieved pleased because your worry has been taken away

to **rely on** to need somebody or something and not be able to work well without them; to depend on

a **remedy** something that solves a problem

remote control using equipment to control something, e.g. a TV from a distance

to **represent** to be equal to

a **resident** a person who lives in a certain place

to be **responsible for** to have the job of taking care of or doing something. Also *to carry responsibility* – having to make decisions about something and be blamed if something goes wrong

to **restore** to put something back into its original condition

to **retire** to stop working at the end of a career, usually at about sixty

revenues total income from sales; turnover

a **reward** something given in return for work, effort, etc. Also *to reward*

to **rocket** to increase very quickly

the **root** the cause or source of something

to **run out of** something to finish your supply of something

to **run to** to add up to; to total

a **salary** regular payment for doing a job

a **scheme** a system for organizing or doing something

to **scrap** to dispose of something that you don't want anymore

a **segment** a section or part of something

a **server** a computer that controls information which can be shared by a group of connected computers

to **set** someone/something **back** to delay someone or something

shape physical outline; a form

a **share** one of the equal parts into which the ownership of a company is divided. Also a *shareholder* – someone who owns shares

to **shelve** to decide not to continue with a plan

a **ship date** the date on which a product is shipped

a **short cut** a quicker, easier, or more direct way to do something

in **short supply** a situation where there isn't enough of something

to **shrink** to get smaller

simultaneously at the same time

to **single out** to choose someone for special attention

a **skill** the ability to do something well, especially because of training, etc. Also *skilled* – having the ability and knowledge to do something well

a **sliding scale** a chart that makes one quantity dependent on another, so they increase or decrease together

a **slogan** a short phrase used in advertising that is easy to remember

smart having intelligence

a **spot** a particular place. Also *on the spot* – at the same time and place as something else that's just happened

to **stack** to put things neatly in a pile

to **stand out** to be different and therefore noticeable

a **startup** a new company

state-owned belonging to a country or its government

a **step** one action in a series of actions

stock shares in a company that people can buy and sell

a **stopover** a short stop between parts of a long journey

a **strategy** a plan you use in order to achieve something

a **strength** a strong point

a **struggle** a fight; a great effort

to **submit** to propose something so it can be discussed

a **subsidiary** a company controlled by another company

a **surcharge** an extra amount of money that you have to pay for something

to **surrender** to stop fighting and admit that you have lost

to **survive** to continue to live

to **swap** to exchange

a **SWOT analysis** (abbreviation) **s**trengths, **w**eaknesses, **o**pportunities, and **t**hreats. A business tool for examining the interaction between a particular business or product and its marketplace

to **tackle** to deal boldly with something difficult, e.g. a problem

tactful careful not to say or do things that could offend people

talented showing natural skill or ability

to **tend to** do something to do something normally or often

theft the crime of taking something that belongs to another person secretly and without permission

a **threat** something that may damage or hurt. Also *to threaten* – to warn that you may damage or hurt; *under threat* – at risk

tight not having much spare time, space, or money

tightly-knit close

top-traded traded the most

tough difficult; hard

on **track** to have done the amount that was planned by a point in time

a **trade fair** a business or industrial exhibition

a **transaction** a piece of business; a business deal or agreement

to **transform** to change something

to **translate** to change something from one language to another. Also *a translator* – someone who translates something that is written

to **transplant** to take something from one place and put it in another

a **trend** a general movement or change

to **turn down** to refuse or reject an offer

unique unlike anything else, being the only one of its type

unless if not

unlimited not restricted; as much as you want

to be **up to** something to be doing something unknown – and possibly something bad

to **update** to report on the current state of things

to **upgrade** to improve or raise the standard of something

urgent needing immediate attention. Also *a sense of urgency* – a feeling that things should be dealt with immediately

VAT (abbreviation) Value Added Tax

a **vehicle** something which transports people or things from place to place

a **venture capitalist** someone who provides the money a startup company needs, usually in return for stock

on the **verge of** doing something very near to doing something; the start of something

viable will be successful; will work

virtual seeming real, although it's produced by pictures and sounds from a computer

visible can be seen or noticed

visual aid charts, maps, etc., used in presentations to help people understand information

vital very important or necessary

voluntary done by choice, not because you have to

a **vote** a method of deciding something by asking people to express their choice and finding out what the majority want

wages payment for doing a job, usually paid weekly to manual workers

wear long use which damages the quality of something

well-rounded having a wide range of knowledge and abilities

well-run well-managed

wide open easy to enter, e.g. *a wide open market* – a market with no competition

to **work** something **out** to find the answer to something

worth the amount of something that an amount of money will buy, e.g. *7 billion dollars' worth*. Also *to be worth it* – sensible and justified, even if it means extra expense or cost

wrapped up finished

OXFORD
UNIVERSITY PRESS

Great Clarendon Street, Oxford OX2 6DP

Oxford University Press is a department of the University of Oxford. It furthers the University's objective of excellence in research, scholarship, and education by publishing worldwide in

Oxford New York

Athens Auckland Bangkok Bogotá Buenos Aires Cape Town Chennai Dar es Salaam Delhi Florence Hong Kong Istanbul Karachi Kolkata Kuala Lumpur Madrid Melbourne Mexico City Mumbai Nairobi Paris São Paulo Shanghai Singapore Taipei Tokyo Toronto Warsaw

with associated companies in Berlin Ibadan

Oxford and Oxford English are registered trade marks of Oxford University Press in the UK and in certain other countries

Acknowledgements

The author and publisher are grateful to those who have given permission to reproduce the following extracts and adaptations of copyright material:

p 7 Information about 3M from www.mmm.com. Reproduced by permission of 3M United Kingdom plc.
p 7 Information about Toyota. Reproduced by permission of Toyota.
p 8 'Hamer Guitars Factory Tour'. From www.edromanguitars.com. Reproduced by permission of Ed Roman Guitars.
p 19 '100 greatest inventions'. Appeared in Focus Magazine May 1997. Reproduced by permission of Focus Magazine.
p 21 'Business Behaviour' from www.williamsinference.com. Reproduced by permission of Williams Inference Center.
p 23 Fantastic Facts by John May. Published by Carlton Books Ltd. Reproduced by permission of Carlton Books Ltd.
p 26 'My greatest lesson – what if (Gorillas in the mist)' by Anna Muolo. Appeared in Fast Company June 1998, Issue 15. Reproduced by permission of Fast Company.
pp 48, 49 'Close Calls' by Cheryl Dahle. Appeared in Fast Company February 1998, Issue 13. Reproduced by permission of Fast Company.
pp 52, 62 'Power to the people' by Alex Markels. Appeared in Fast Company February 1998, Issue 13. Reproduced by permission of Fast Company.

pp 52, 62 'Going global is a long journey' by Alex Markels. Appeared in Fast Company February 1998, Issue 13. Reproduced by permission of Fast Company.
p 27 Film producer's story – Phelps Dodge Copper Corporation. Reproduced by permission of DBS Films, Inc.
p 28 'The 100 best companies to work for' by Robert Levering and Milton Moskowitz. From Fortune Magazine 10 January 2000. © 2000 Time Inc. Reproduced by permission of Time Life Syndication.
pp 40, 46, 60 Extracts from www.disruptivetechnologies.com. Reproduced by permission of Integral Inc (Tel. USA 617-349-0600).
p 54 Extracts from Riding the Waves of Culture by Fons Trompenaars. Reproduced by permission of Nicholas Brealy Publishing.
p 10 Information about Dana Corporation from www.dana.com. Reproduced by permission of Dana Corporation.
p 7 Information about FedEx Express. Reproduced by permission of FedEx Express.
p 44 Information about Energy E-Comm.com. Reproduced by permission of Frederick H. Abrew, Chairman.
Sources:
p 29 From 'Rising staff turnover: How UK business is responding'. Published by Reed Personnel Services.

Illustrations by:
Sarah Jones: p 14
Nigel Paige: pp 1, 15, 23, 45, 46

The publisher would like to thank the following for their kind permission to reproduce photographs:
Corbis: pp 34 (Rio de Janeiro), 35 (Rome); Eye Ubiquitous: pp 37 (long-life bulb, loft insulation/Paul Seheult), 52 (power station/Julia Waterlow); FedEx p 6 (FedEx employee); Frederick H. Abrew p 44 (portrait); Hamer p 8 (Hamer guitar production); Harvard University p 62 (Clayton Christensen); Image Bank p 21 (businessman asleep/S. Krongard); Kobal p 26 (Gorillas in the Mist/Michael Apted); Photodisc: pp 34 (Honolulu, Singapore, Beijing), 35 (Moscow), 48 (streetsign); Powerstock/Zefa p36 (wind farm); Stone: pp cover (business men walking/Leland Bobbe) 19 (optical bench/Bob Thomason), 33 (airport counter/J P Williams), 35 (Bombay/Alan Smith), 51 and cover (business executives/John Lamb), 60 (computer terminal/Stephen Johnson); Telegraph Colour Library: pp 5 and cover (executives shaking hands/R Chapple), 10 and cover (business meeting), 19 (Microchips/Stuart Hunter, laser technology/Seth Joel, laser beams through hands/VCL), 25 (car production/Barry Willis), 40 (steel works/Neal Wilson), 42 (clock heads in desert/J Porto/FPG) 55 (business colleagues meeting/Chris Ryan/VCL); 3M p 6 (business stationery); Tografox (solar panels/R. D. Battersby); Toyota 6 (Toyota workers); Photodisc cover (train)

Commissioned photography by:
David Tolley: pp 5 (conference, airport, trade fair), 13 (presenter), 17 (brainstorming session)

Designed by Shireen Nathoo Design, London

The author and publisher would also like to thank the following individuals for their help and advice in the preparation of this book:

The staff and students at EF Corporate Executive Language Schools in Cambridge, UK and Boston, USA, and ELP at the University of Pennsylvania, USA.